T0340991

Paint with Needle and Thread

A Step-by-Step Guide to **Chinese Embroidery**

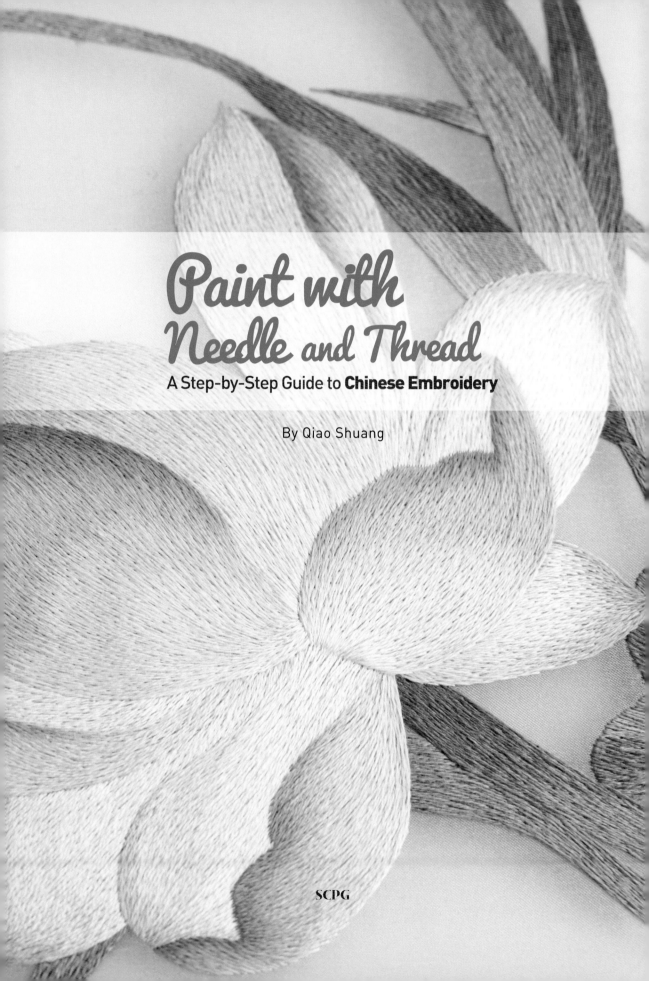

Paint with
Needle and Thread
A Step-by-Step Guide to **Chinese Embroidery**

By Qiao Shuang

SCPG

On page 1
Fig. 1 The *Kingfisher* embroidered with silk threads. Find and embroider the same project using cotton threads on page 207.

On pages 2–3
Fig. 2 Detail of *The Lotus* (see page 201).

Bottom
Fig. 3 The silk embroidery of flowers and leaves (by the author).

On page 5, above
Fig. 4 The silk embroidery of Chinese landscape painting (by the author).

On page 5, bottom
Fig. 5 The silk embroidery of traditional floral scrolls pattern (by the author).

Text: Qiao Shuang
Photography: Zhou Feiyu
Digital Drawing: Hong Jiaxin

Translation: Shelly Bryant
Cover Design: Shi Hanlin
Interior Design: Hu Bin, Li Jing (Yuan Yinchang Design Studio)

Editor: Wu Yuezhou
Assistant Editor: Qiu Yan

ISBN: 978-1-63288-000-0

Address any comments about *Paint with Needle and Thread: A Step-by-Step Guide to Chinese Embroidery* to:

SCPG
401 Broadway, Ste. 1000
New York, NY 10013
USA

or

Shanghai Press and Publishing Development Co., Ltd.
Floor 5, No. 390 Fuzhou Road, Shanghai, China (200001)
Email: sppd@sppdbook.com

Printed in China by Shanghai Donnelley Printing Co., Ltd.

1   3   5   7   9   10   8   6   4   2

CONTENTS

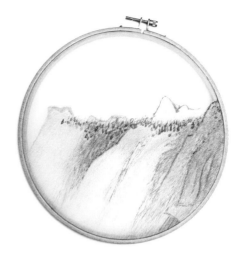

CONTENTS

On facing page
Fig. 6   This artwork of *Butterfly in Love with Flowers* is embroidered with silk threads. For the same project embroidered with cotton threads, please refer to page 187.

Right
Fig. 7   Embroidery of flowers finished with knot stitch technique (by the author).

Fig. 8 Guang embroidery of flowers and birds of Qing dynasty (1644–1911).

CHAPTER ONE
Ancient and Modern Chinese Embroidery

Chinese embroidery has a long history spanning thousands of years. From primitive societies to the present day, Chinese women's delicate hands have used needle and thread to accumulate, improve, and create countless artistic treasures.

In this long history, Chinese embroidery has developed two distinct paths: decorative embroidery and appreciative embroidery. These two types of embroidery have collectively shaped the high level and wide-ranging scope of Chinese embroidery, showcasing its artistic essence and vitality and exerting a profound influence on other countries as well.

1. The Grand Tradition of Chinese Embroidery

Embroidery is one of China's oldest traditional crafts, possibly originating from the ancient customs of painting or tattooing. According to the important text *Shangshu*, written around 3,000 years ago, the history of Chinese embroidery can be traced back to the era of the Three Sovereigns and Five Emperors (approximately 25th century BC to 21st century BC). Emperor Shun established twelve patterns that were used to decorate clothing through painting and embroidery techniques. These twelve patterns symbolize the emperor's role as the bearer of all things in the universe, and the tradition of embroidering these twelve designs on the most prestigious imperial robes was passed down for thousands of years until the end of the imperial system in China. In other words, the twelve patterns that symbolize royal authority and hierarchical status was recorded in the important ancient Chinese classic as early as 3,000 years ago. And these patterns were embroidered using colorful threads (fig. 9).

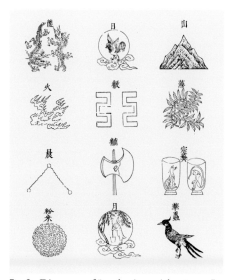

Fig. 9 Diagrams of "twelve imperial patterns."

Fig. 10 The chain stitch imprints found in a Western Zhou dynasty tomb in Rujia Village, Baoji, Shaanxi Province, dating back to the pre-Qin era.

Fig. 11 A phoenix bird embroidered pattern on a coffin cover excavated from a Western Zhou dynasty tomb in Jiang County, Shanxi Province, dating back to the pre-Qin era.

As of now, the earliest evidence of embroidery discovered in China comes from the tomb of Fu Hao in Anyang, Henan Province. Fu Hao was a queen during the Shang dynasty (1600–1046 BC). In her tomb, a bronze vessel was found with embroidery imprints in the form of diamond patterns, an artifact currently housed in the Museum of Far Eastern Antiquities in Sweden. Archaeological excavations of two Western Zhou dynasty (1046–771 BC) tombs also revealed evidence of chain stitch and satin stitch. These findings provide further historical proof of the embroidery techniques used during that period (figs. 10 and 11).

Due to their delicate nature, textiles with embroidery are prone to decay in tombs and are difficult to preserve for as long as materials such as metal, stone, jade, wood, and lacquer. As a result, a large number of embroidered artifacts have disappeared into the depths of history. However, it is certain that the history of Chinese embroidery extends far beyond what can be reliably documented. For thousands of years, the art of embroidery has been closely intertwined with the lives and customs of the Chinese people, and it has been used to express their aspirations and prayers for a better life, making it one of China's most treasured cultural heritages.

Early Period

During the Shang and Zhou periods (1600–256 BC), China developed into a class-based society, with specialized artisans engaged in various handicrafts and creations to cater to the luxurious lifestyle of the nobility. Embroidery was one of the art forms practiced during this period. According to records, during the reign of King Zhou of Shang, hundreds of women in the palace were adorned in clothing embroidered with intricate patterns. Even the walls and furniture in the palace were embellished with embroidered textiles. During the Western Zhou period, the society and economy continued to develop further compared to the Shang dynasty. Crafts such as weaving, dyeing, and embroidery had specialized divisions of labor. Historical records also contained more detailed accounts of embroidery during this time. For example, the *Rites of Zhou* specifically recorded the colors and techniques of combining painting with embroidery.

The Spring and Autumn period (770–476 BC) and the Warring States period (475–221 BC) were marked by political fragmentation and frequent warfare. However, there was also significant political interaction among the various states, leading to the development of trade and exchange of goods and technologies. As a result, the people's lifestyle became increasingly luxurious, and they enjoyed more comforts and extravagance during this era. Not only did the monarchs of the times wear garments adorned with exquisite embroidery, but they also bestowed whole pieces of silk fabric embroidered with elegance as rewards to their ministers. Their attendants wear embroidered clothing, and even their beloved horses had embroidered adornments on their caparisons. During that time, the nobles enjoy luxurious embroidered items even followed them in death, as their coffins were draped with intricately embroidered textiles. Dragon and phoenix patterns using chain stitch have been found on the coffins of Warring States period Chu tombs unearthed in Changsha, Hunan Province.

From the Qin dynasty (221–206 BC) unification of China to the Han dynasty (206 BC–AD 220), over a period of nearly 450 years, handicrafts underwent a period of recovery and development. The state even established dedicated embroidery workshops to produce embroidered goods, catering to the lifestyle needs of the imperial family and nobility. During the Han dynasty, there was a wide variety of embroidery products, and embroidery was practiced in various regions across the country. Folk embroidery techniques were well-developed in some areas. Embroidered products, once exclusive to monarchs and nobles, became accessible to wealthy landowners and merchants during that time. Embroidery became a common decorative method in clothing and living spaces. Appreciation and use of embroidered items became a popular hobby. The popularity of this trend grew to the extent that even the highest rulers had to implement restrictive measures.

From the unearthed artifacts, it can be observed that various embroidery techniques such as the chain stitch, satin stitch, knot stitch, and regular shaded satin stitch had appeared in China by the Han dynasty. However, throughout the span of over 1,800 years from the Shang dynasty to the Han dynasty, chain stitch remained the dominant embroidery method. Based on the embroidery artifacts discovered to date, the vast majority of them have been completed using chain stitch technique. The craftsmanship is exquisite, showcasing magnificent, intricate decorative patterns on clothing and textiles.

From a craftsmanship perspective, the chain stitch can effectively depict continuous winding lines. It can also be used to fill patterns with interlocking circles, and even create the fading effect by changing the color of silk threads. The chain stitch was highly suitable for portraying the decorative patterns of the Shang, Zhou, Qin, and Han periods, where patterns were outlined with lines and filled with colored blocks. Its unique needlework enriched the visual effect of the patterns, making them both visually appealing and durable, and its practicality and resistance to wear and washing have contributed to its widespread usage in folk embroidery even to this day.

Mature Period

Chinese embroidery craftsmanship continued to develop during the Wei, Jin, and the Northern and Southern dynasties (220–589), undergoing a period of innovation and transformation. The period of Wei, Jin, and the Northern and Southern dynasties was characterized by frequent changes of political power. Five different ethnic groups established separate states during this time. On one hand, there were constant wars and conflicts; on the other hand, for various political and military reasons, there were population migrations and cultural exchanges between the north and south. The increasing frequency of cultural exchange between the east and the west through the Silk Road led to a diverse cultural fusion as well, which infused the art of embroidery with new elements in terms of patterns, colors, materials, and techniques. Especially with the rise of Buddhism, the use of embroidery expanded significantly. There was a high demand for embroidery in temple decorations, embroidering Buddha statues, and producing Buddhist paraphernalia. This shift in demand transformed embroidery from simple pattern work to more complex representations, such as human figures. It gave birth to new breakthroughs in embroidery techniques and forms of expression.

Many of the unearthed embroidery artifacts from the Wei, Jin, and the Northern and Southern dynasties are related to Buddhism. Although the number of surviving pieces is not large, they are exceptionally exquisite in craftsmanship. The colored embroidery fragments of Buddha statues and devotee

Fig. 12   A Northern Wei embroidery depicting a Buddha statue and a devotee offering, unearthed from the Mogao Grottoes (Caves 125 to 126) in Dunhuang, Gansu Province.

offerings discovered in the Mogao Grottoes in Dunhuang from the Northern Wei (386–534) period are the earliest known colored embroidery of Buddha statues to date (fig. 12). They are also the earliest surviving examples of decorative needle painting artwork. They mark the beginning of China's world-renowned needle painting (*hua xiu* or embroidered painting), a form of embroidery primarily for artistic appreciation, using stitching to depict paintings. From this point until the Song dynasty (960–1279), the subject of embroidery shifted from patterns to paintings. As Chinese figure painting and bird-and-flower painting became more sophisticated, the demand for realistic representation in embroidery also increased. This led to the diversification and maturation of embroidery techniques.

After nearly 300 years of division, the large fragmented landscape of China was unified by the Sui dynasty (581–618), leading to one of the best known dynasties in Chinese history, the Tang dynasty (618–907). During the Tang dynasty, there was significant development in politics, culture, and the economy. Diplomatic and trade activities with the western regions and various East Asian countries were frequent, leading to unprecedented levels of cultural exchange and fusion between east and west. During the Tang dynasty, the style of embroidery was vigorous, full-bodied, and splendid, radiating a lively, vibrant atmosphere. The patterns of embroidery were influenced by western styles during the Tang dynasty, making the designs

Fig. 13 *Shakyamuni Preaching* embroidered painting, housed in the Nara National Museum, Japan, with its detail on the right.

Fig. 14 *Queen Mother on a Crane* needle painting, housed in the Liaoning Provincial Museum.

more diverse and rich in variety. The further prosperity of Buddhism and the diversification of decorations during the Tang dynasty contributed to the enrichment of embroidery techniques (see fig. 13 on page 13). During the Tang dynasty, on one hand, chain stitch technique was still extensively used and executed with exceptional skill. On the other hand, new techniques such as satin stitch, basic encroaching satin stitch, encroaching satin stitch with hidden threads, split stitch, backstitch, shaded satin stitch and blended stitch emerged, laying an important foundation for the future development of embroidery. During the Tang dynasty, the art of *cujin* embroidery, which involved using gold threads, emerged. In later periods, it was divided into two styles: *panjin* (gold thread couching stitch) and *pingjin* (goldwork embroidery). Due to its dazzling, luxurious appearance, *cujin* embroidery was widely utilized by the imperial family and nobility in their ceremonial garments as a decorative element. This tradition continued even until the Qing dynasty (1644–1911).

Reaching the Realm of Sublimation: The Development of Needle Painting

The Song dynasty, one of the most prosperous periods in Chinese history, was characterized by a thriving commodity economy and flourishing culture and education. During this period, painting reached a refined, highly developed state, which also had an influence on the field of embroidery. Under the patronage of the upper classes, needle painting emerged as a distinct form of embroidery, specializing in imitating paintings and calligraphy for artistic appreciation. It gradually separated itself from practical embroidery techniques. As needle painting aimed to achieve effects close to traditional painting, it led to further refinement of embroidery techniques that had already developed since the Tang dynasty. During this period, embroidery became even more delicate and intricate, with a richer color palette and smoother color transitions, showcasing the exquisite, skillful craftsmanship of embroidery. The famous Song dynasty needle painting, *Queen Mother on a Crane*, utilized extremely fine silk threads to combine more than a dozen embroidery techniques such as the satin, blended, stem, knot, couching, gold thread couching, and goldwork embroidery stitches. These techniques, along with the use of painted backgrounds, created an elegant, refined representation of a painting through embroidery, displaying exquisite attention to detail (fig. 14).

During the Song dynasty, there were significant explorations in needle paintings, and the form reached its peak during the Ming dynasty (1368–1644). One of the most famous achievements was the art of Gu embroidery, which continued to flourish even into the Qing dynasty. Gu embroidery, named after the Gu family in Shanghai, produced several outstanding female embroidery artists during the Ming dynasty. Their works imitated ancient paintings with meticulous craftsmanship and attention to detail. These artists did not keep track of the costs involved and often created their pieces for

Fig. 15 The needle painting of *Fish*, embroidered by Han Ximeng.

personal collections or as gifts for family and friends, rather than for commercial purposes. Gu embroidery was considered the finest embroidery of the Ming dynasty (fig. 15). In particular, the Gu family's daughter-in-law, Han Ximeng, excelled in embroidering landscape and bird-and-flower painting albums, which gained the admiration and praise of renowned scholar and painter Dong Qichang (1555–1636). His recognition elevated Han Ximeng's embroidery to the literati circle and played a crucial role in the development and promotion of needle paintings during that era. By the end of the Ming dynasty, the Gu family's influence declined, and the talented female members of the Gu family began teaching their exquisite embroidery techniques. This led to the spread of Gu embroidery to regions like Jiangsu and laid the foundation for the next peak of Chinese needle paintings.

During the Qing dynasty, the art of embroidery saw significant development based on the foundation laid during the Ming dynasty. Embroidered items created for imperial use reached a peak in terms of skill and quantity. Additionally, commercial embroidery became extremely popular, leading to the emergence of specialized embroidery workshops in various regions. This gradually gave rise to distinct regional embroidery systems. The four famous styles of embroidery—Su embroidery (Jiangsu), Guang embroidery (Guangdong) (see fig. 8 on page 8), Shu embroidery (Sichuan), and Xiang embroidery (Hunan)—all came into existence during this period, showcasing the flourishing development of folk embroidery.

An exceptional embroidery artist named Shen Shou (1874–1921) worked in the late Qing period. Upon seeing Western oil paintings that differed greatly from the traditional Chinese painting style, emphasizing light, shadow, and three-dimensionality, she creatively employed various embroidery stitching techniques. She pioneered a style called realistic embroidery, which could intricately reproduce the subjects depicted in oil paintings and photographs, achieving an astonishing level of detail and lifelikeness. In 1911, she completed

Fig. 16 Shen Shou's *Portrait of Jesus*.

Fig. 17 Yang Shouyu's *Portrait of a Young Lady* using alternating stitch.

the embroidery portrait titled *Portrait of Italian Empress Elena*, which was presented as a state gift to Italy, causing a sensation. The Italian emperor and empress personally corresponded with the Qing government, praising the exquisite artistry of Suzhou embroidery in China. They also displayed this artwork at the Turin International Exposition in Italy, where it received the Supreme Award of World's Greatest Honor for its exceptional achievement. In 1915, she embroidered the *Portrait of Jesus* (fig. 16) and participated in the Panama-Pacific International Exposition held in San Francisco, California, USA. Her work received the first-place prize at the exhibition. The embroidery techniques she pioneered were inherited and improved by numerous embroidery artists after the founding of the People's Republic of China. Eventually, these innovations pushed China's embroidery skills to the realm where virtually anything could be depicted through embroidery.

Following Shen Shou, another embroidery master emerged, Yang Shouyu (1896–1981). Influenced by Western sketching and Impressionist painting during her youth, she pioneered a new style of embroidery called alternating stitch embroidery, which expanded the techniques and styles of embroidery painting. Today, alternating stitch embroidery has become a significant, indispensable means of artistic expression and a distinctive style within the realm of appreciative embroidery in China (fig. 17).

Fig. 18 Embroidery on Ming dynasty's official robes.

2. Unique Manifestation of Chinese Aesthetics

With its long history, vast territory, and amalgamation of diverse ethnic groups, along with the exchange between Chinese and Western cultures, Chinese embroidery has developed a rich, complex appearance. However, overall, it can be divided into three types based on their historical emergence: 1) embroidery for royal service, 2) embroidery used by common people in their daily life, and 3) appreciative embroidery paintings cherished by the literati and scholar-official class. The embroidery art across these three areas collectively presents the unique aesthetics of Chinese embroidery.

Royal Embroidery

Embroidery on garments and items exclusively used by the royal family, nobility, and even officials served not only decorative purposes but also primarily functioned to distinguish social classes and identities, aiding in political governance. The legend of the Yellow Emperor "dropping his robe and bringing order to the country" illustrates how the emperor's ceremonial attire had the function of demonstrating his identity and assisting in governance. Emperor Shun's establishment of the twelve embroidered patterns on the emperor's ceremonial attire further emphasized the political significance of embroidery decoration. In later generations, the emperor's robes were adorned with dragon motifs, while phoenix motifs were reserved for the empress. After specific regulations were established regarding the number and design of dragon and phoenix patterns that members of the royal family of different ranks could use, the function of embroidery patterns in defining hierarchy and status became even more distinct. Furthermore, in China, official robes for government officials used distinct patterns to clearly differentiate between civil officials, military officials, and different ranks of officials. As a result, the aesthetic appeal and innovation of such embroidery patterns were constrained by the political demands that were passed down through successive generations. However, the enduring patterns and symbols that have remained stable for thousands of years, representing the dignity, opulence, and intricacy associated with royal prestige, have also formed an iconic representation of nobility and elegance within Chinese embroidery (fig. 18).

Folk Embroidery

Decorative embroidery used in the daily life of ancient common people often conformed to folk customs and carried auspicious meanings. For example, in folk culture, when women embroidered *hebao* (a small purse as an accessory that could be carried around) for their lovers, they often chose patterns of mandarin ducks playing in water, symbolizing the wish for a lifelong partnership and companionship (fig. 19). Another example is the embroidery on bellybands given to children during the Dragon Boat Festival, often featuring patterns of the Five Poisonous Creatures (snake, lizard, scorpion, toad, centipede), believed to ward off illnesses and disasters. From a young age, women would begin embroidering their own wedding garments. A set of richly embroidered bridal trousseau, handcrafted by the bride herself, showcased her talents. The patterns embroidered on the wedding garments often included auspicious symbols like the characters for 福 (*fu*, good fortune) and 喜 (*xi*, happiness), as well as motifs like mandarin ducks, pomegranates,

Fig. 19 Embroidered pouch with auspicious meaning.

and peonies, symbolizing wishes for a harmonious and blessed marriage, longevity, and fertility. With the gradual removal of restrictions on embroidery pattern hierarchy, dragons and phoenixes became even more prominent as the key decorative motifs on festive garments.

China is one of the few countries in the world with a diverse range of ethnicities. Apart from the Han ethnicity, various minority groups have their own unique mythologies, folk customs, and even distinct embroidery patterns that serve as symbols of their respective cultures. In regions with a diverse mix of ethnicities, the embroidery patterns on clothing have become crucial symbols for individuals to express and identify with their respective ethnic backgrounds. For instance, among the Yao ethnic group, there is a longstanding legend about the Yao King's seal. Yao girls embroider the pattern of the seal held by their tribal king onto their clothing to signify their Yao identity. Similarly, within a branch

Fig. 20 Details of embroidered clothes of Miao ethnic group.

of the Miao ethnic group, during a historical migration, they embroidered an octagonal flower pattern onto their clothing to distinguish their ethnic group and make it easier for companions to identify each other (fig. 20).

Chinese folk embroidery is characterized by its freedom, variability, and richness. For thousands of years, across the vast expanse of China, the diligent, ingenious labor of the people, driven by their aspirations for a better life, have shaped the vivid beauty of Chinese folk embroidery, stitch by stitch.

Appreciative Needle Paintings

Appreciative needle paintings gradually developed alongside the progression of Chinese painting. As Chinese figure painting, bird-and-flower painting, and landscape painting matured over time, skillful educated women in noble families sought to go beyond patterned decorative embroidery. They tightly integrated embroidery with the art of painting, adopting the concept of using needles instead of brushes. This approach aimed to achieve the utmost artistic expression through embroidery. The essence of traditional Chinese painting, which emphasizes the vitality of *qi* and the ambiance of the scene, profoundly influenced the style of needle paintings. This influence gave rise to an elegance distinct from the opulence of the royal court and the vivacity of folk embroidery.

Fig. 21 Embroidered artwork by Zou Yingzi (left).
Fig. 22 Needle painting *Lotus Series* by Liang Xuefang
(above).

3. Exploration of Contemporary Chinese Embroidery

The history of Chinese embroidery has endowed contemporary Chinese embroidery with abundant resources and a profound sense of mission for contemporary artisans. Countless embroidery artists have inherited the ancient techniques, pushing them to even more astonishing heights. Among them, many stand out for their diligent explorations and innovations while upholding tradition. For instance, the renowned Chinese National Master of Arts and Crafts, Ms. Zou Yingzi, delved into the ancient techniques of chain stitch, split stitch, and thread blending and twisting through the meticulous re-embroidery of the Tang dynasty monumental embroidery *Shakyamuni Preaching on Vulture Peak*, now housed in the British Museum. This process led her to rediscover many techniques that had been lost to history. Her own creative works embody an artistry that is both ancient and modern. Another example is Liang Xuefang, a Provincial Master of Arts and Crafts from Jiangsu Province. She has combined contemporary Chinese painting aesthetics with embroidery to create a series of modern needle paintings (figs. 21 and 22).

In today's world, with more convenient cultural and technological exchanges, handicraft exchanges between countries have taken on entirely new forms. In addition to preserving their own embroidery traditions, many young artists and artisans in China are actively learning traditional techniques from other countries, as well as new materials and processes. They are exploring how to integrate these influences with China's embroidery heritage, seeking new developments for this ancient craft in the context of globalization.

CHAPTER TWO
Preparation

T o facilitate understanding and mastery of the techniques and production process used in Chinese embroidery, this chapter introduces the tools, materials, and basic steps involved in the preparation for embroidery work, along with technical terms that will be used in the rest of the book.

1. Materials

The main materials used in Chinese embroidery are the base fabric and the embroidery thread.

Base Fabric

In Chinese embroidery, the effect and techniques applied are determined by the subject matter and content of the image, and the base fabric is then selected accordingly. All sorts of textiles can be used as the base fabric. The base fabrics in traditional Chinese embroidery are usually made of silk, such as silk, satin, tough silk, sheer silk, or silk gauze. These base fabrics are all fine in texture and suitable for delicate embroidery with silk thread. If cotton thread is used for the embroidery, base fabrics such as cotton cloth, cotton linen, and linen should be used as the base fabric.

Most of the embroidery patterns in this book are relatively delicate, embroidered with single-strand cotton thread, and most of the patterns are in the traditional Chinese style, so thin, fine organza has been chosen for the base fabric. Organza is well suited to drawing, and the pattern and edges of the image can be embroidered tightly and neatly, creating clear, elegant embroidered works. Note that the texture of the organza should be fine and dense. Sparse organza will be pulled by the embroidery thread during the needleworking process, and the pinholes will become larger, making the outline of the embroidery difficult to control. For beginners, using cotton as base fabric instead of organza will help you hide the threads on the back much easier.

On facing page
Fig. 23 Details of *Butterfly in Love with Flowers* (see page 187).

Fig. 24 Organza of 8 mm in different colors.

For any type of base fabric you use, be sure to choose one that is not elastic. An elastic fabric will become misshapen when it is stretched, and it will be pulled and warped by the embroidery thread during the needleworking process. When selecting your fabric, pull it both horizontally and vertically. If it can be stretched, it should not be used. A slight stretch when pulled at a 45 degree angle is normal (fig. 24).

Embroidery Thread

The most typical feature of traditional Chinese embroidery is its use of silk thread. Silk embroidery thread is much thinner than cotton threads, and because of the characteristics of its fibers, one thread can be subdivided into 24 strands. Many fine embroideries use 2-strand or 3-strand silks, which is 1/8 or 1/5 of a silk embroidery thread. Clearly, embroidery is very delicate, time-consuming labor (figs. 25 and 26).

Fig. 25 Silk embroidery threads in big bundles.

Fig. 26 Silk embroidery threads in small bundles.

In an effort to make it easier for embroidery enthusiasts to use readily available materials, all the works in this book use mainly cotton embroidery thread. The main threads used are No. 25 embroidery threads from Olympus, DMC, or Anchor. This sort of thread consists of 6-strand threads in a bundle, usually cut into lengths of 20 to 30 cm, which are then pulled out one at a time for use (fig. 27).

In this book, gold thread is used for *panjin* embroidery or gold thread couching stitch, which is thicker than ordinary French embroidery gold thread and has a gorgeous decorative texture when used in embroidery (fig. 28).

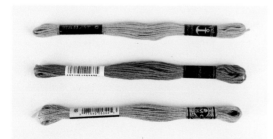

Fig. 27 From top down: embroidery threads from Anchor, Olympus and DMC.

Fig. 28 Gold thread.

2. Tools

The tools needed for embroidery include embroidery hoops, embroidery frames, needles, scissors, and pens, among other things. The tools introduced here include both those for traditional and modern techniques that make the embroidery work more convenient.

Embroidery Hoops

There are two types of embroidery hoops: hoop rings and scroll frames.

Hoop rings are circular hoops made up of an inner and an outer frame. They can be held directly in the hand for embroidery work. The advantage of hoop rings is that they are easy to use and lightweight, making them easy to carry. However, they are only suitable for embroidering small areas. When selecting a hoop ring, it is important to consider the weight if you plan on embroidering for a long time. If the hoop is too heavy, it may cause fatigue in the hand. Additionally, it is important to choose a hoop with a tight grip between the inner and outer frame if you plan to embroider thin fabrics. If the grip is not strong enough, the fabric may move during the embroidery process, causing the embroidery to become warped or wrinkled. To increase the friction between the fabric and the hoop, you can wrap the inner frame with a ribbon or cloth. Hoop rings come in various sizes, and it is best to choose one that is larger than the embroidery design to prevent the embroidery from becoming warped when changing positions (figs. 29 and 30).

Fig. 29 Hoop rings of 12 cm, 15 cm and 18 cm in diameter.

Fig. 30 Hoop ring with webbing wrapped around the inner frame.

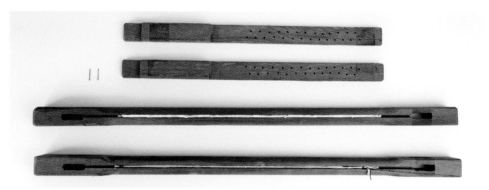

Fig. 31 Chinese embroidery scroll frames.

Fig. 32 French embroidery scroll frames.

Scroll frames are generally rectangular frames made up of two wooden sticks, one on each side of the fabric. The two horizontal sticks are used to connect the embroidery fabric. Traditional Chinese scroll frames have rectangular ends on both horizontal sticks, and the middle section is cylindrical with a fine groove. This groove can hold a thin strip of wood that secures the fabric. Since most Chinese embroidery uses lightweight silk or other thin fabrics, thicker cotton fabric is sewn onto the top and bottom of the embroidery fabric to increase friction, and then the thick cotton fabric is placed in the groove and secured with a strip of wood (fig. 31).

French embroidery scroll frames have two horizontally elongated rectangular sticks with thick, stiff ribbons nailed on top to sew the embroidery fabric. The left and right sticks of both Chinese and French scroll frames serve the same purpose of pulling and tightening the embroidery fabric. There are nails or screws on both sides of the sticks that fix the horizontal bar. Additionally, using slightly thicker thread, rope, or ribbon, the fabric can be tightened and fixed on both sides of the sticks, ensuring that the fabric is completely flat and taut. Although there are different design details in Chinese and French scroll frames, the basic principle is the same: to flatten a large piece of fabric for embroidery. You can also use the French embroidery hoop method and use pins with herringbone ribbon instead of the thick cotton thread for fixing (fig. 32).

Embroidery Stand

There are embroidery stands that can be used together with hoop rings and scroll frames.

Traditional Chinese hoop rings do not have embroidery stands, but with the development of handicrafts and the integration of embroidery tools and materials from various countries, embroidery stands that free up hands with hoop rings have been introduced. One is a embroidery stand, similar to a clamp that can fix a hoop ring, including desktop embroidery stands that can be placed on a table and table-clamp embroidery stands that can fix a hoop ring to the edge of a table. The other type is an integrated embroidery stand that is connected to the hoop ring. There are also seated embroidery stands and table-clamp embroidery stands that can be fixed to the edge of a table (figs. 33–35).

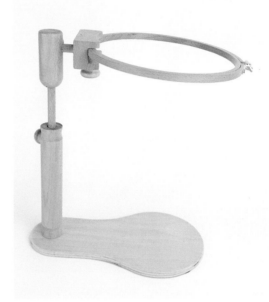

Fig. 33   Embroidery stand on table.

Scroll embroidery hoops are relatively large and cannot be directly placed on a table for use, so they generally need to be used with a special embroidery frame. Traditional Chinese embroidery frames generally have three legs, two of which form a pair, placed on the outside of the legs, where the scrolls can

Fig. 34   Plastic embroidery hoop stand wtih table clamp.

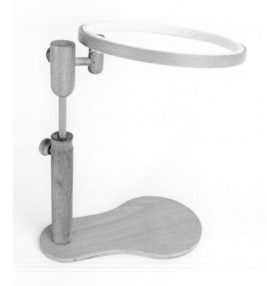

Fig. 35   Embroidery stand on lap.

Fig. 36 Traditional Chinese embroidery frame stands.

Fig. 37 Adjustable table legs.

be placed flat on the top (fig. 36). You can also choose adjustable table legs and adjust them to your own height and preferences (fig. 37).

Scissors

Scissors for cutting fabric in embroidery are sharp professional scissors that should not be used for anything other than cutting fabric, otherwise, the blades will be easily damaged. If cutting thin silk fabrics, professional silk scissors can also be used (figs. 38 and 39).

Thread-cutting scissors should be small, sharp, and have a pointed tip, preferably bent, to cut the thread close to the surface of the embroidery (figs. 40 and 41).

Fig. 38 Scissors used for cutting fabrics.

Fig. 39 Scissors with serration on the edge, used for cutting silk.

Fig. 40 Small and sharp scissors.

Fig. 41 Scissors with curved tip.

Embroidery Needle

Because they need to be used with silk embroidery thread to make extremely fine embroidery, traditional Chinese embroidery needles are very thin and have small eyes. Today, popular embroidery is mostly done with cotton thread and often uses double-strand, triple-strand, or even six-strand threads for embroidery. Therefore, it is also necessary to prepare embroidery needles of different sizes for different needle eyes. Generally, two sets of needles can be prepared. One set is needles of different sizes from fine to thick (fig. 42), and the other set is fine needles of the same type (fig. 43).

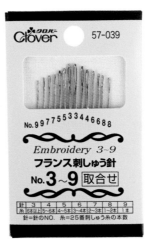

Fig. 42 A set of embroidery needles from fine to thick.

Fig. 43 A set of fine embroidery needles for single-strand threads.

Because fine needles are used the most, when embroidering multiple colors, to save time on changing threads, several different colored threads can be threaded onto separate needles and used in turn.

Others

Threading the needle is a frequent operation in embroidery. A **needle threader** can help easily thread the small needle eye. It can also easily thread multiple strands of thread at the same time. The red one on the left is the threader for fine threads, the green one on the right is the threader for multi-stranded or thick threads.

The tip of the **seam ripper** can pick up the wrong stitches, and the sharp blade at the concave part can easily remove large areas of embroidered errors. It is more convenient and safer than using scissors for removing mistakes. When using the seam ripper, be careful not to pierce the base fabric and ensure that the seam ripper is inserted between the fabric and the thread.

When doing embroidery, many needles are often used, and sometimes sewing pins are also used. To prevent the needles from getting lost, it is necessary to always store them on a **pin cushion**. When embroidering patterns with gradient colors, it is often necessary to use three or more embroidery threads for the transition. To save time and avoid wasting thread, it is better to thread each embroidery thread onto a different needle and switch between them instead of repeatedly changing the thread on the same needle. When making delicate transitions, the thread colors are often very similar. In such instances, you can arrange the needles with the threaded embroidery threads in order of the color number. This will prevent confusion and save embroidery time.

Ball head pins (above) and flat head pins (bottom) can be used to secure the pattern and fabric. For small patterns, you can draw directly onto the fabric, and for large patterns, you can use sewing pins to secure the fabric and then sew around the edge to fix it in place. After removing the pins, you can draw on the fabric.

Many Chinese embroideries use silk or thin gauze as the base fabric, so when tracing a pattern, the drawing is usually placed and fixed on the back of the base fabric. If the fabric is slightly thicker or thinner cotton fabric is light in color, you can use a **light box** to light up the back of the fabric to clearly see the pattern and trace it. If the cotton fabric is dark in color, you can adjust the pattern on the computer to have a black background and white lines and then use a light box to trace it. This method allows you to draw a clear pattern directly on the fabric without tarnishing the front.

If you don't have a light box, you can use a light under a glass table or stick the paper onto a window and use sunlight or a light to trace the pattern.

When using thick, dark fabric, even with a tracing light box, it may be difficult to trace the pattern clearly. In such cases, you can use **transfer paper for fabric**, which is white in color, to trace the pattern. Place the transfer paper on the front of the fabric, then place the pattern on top and secure everything in place. Then, you can trace the pattern onto the fabric using a tracing tool. The downside of using transfer paper is that it may smudge the fabric, and you cannot see the pattern while tracing, which may result in misplaced or missing elements.

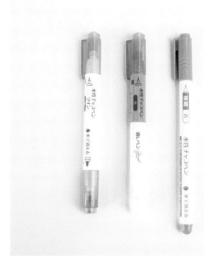

Heat erasable pens can easily draw patterns on the base fabric, after completing the embroidery, heating the pattern with a hair dryer or iron can erase it. If hand-stretched embroidery is done on a larger scale, it is not suitable to use a heat erasable pen because when you change the hand-stretching position, the wrinkled part of the fabric needs to be ironed flat, which will erase the heated part of the pattern. Heat erasable pens come in various colors and can be selected based on the color of the fabric to create a contrasting effect. A 0.5 mm pen is generally suitable for tracing.

The patterns drawn by **water erasable pens** will not be erased by heat, so if ironing is required during the embroidery process, a water erasable pen can be used to draw the pattern. The marks made by high-quality water erasable pens can be completely erased by gently wetting them with water or by using the pen's own eraser head. Water erasable pens are also suitable for tracing because they allow for easy correction of any mistakes made.

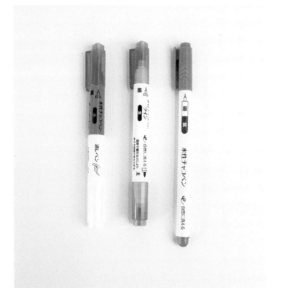

Air erasable pens are a type of pen that uses the moisture in the air to erase the marks it makes. The advantage of using air erasable pens is that they do not require special erasing, but their marks generally only last for 3 to 5 days. Therefore, they can be used to trace works that will be completed within two or three days or to make some temporary markings. If you want to immediately clear the marks made by air erasable pens, you can simply wet them with water.

Iron pens are tools used in conjunction with transfer paper for fabric. Iron pens are like pens that do not have ink, with a pointed tip that can draw clear lines during the drawing process without worrying about the ink leaking onto the fabric like a regular pen.

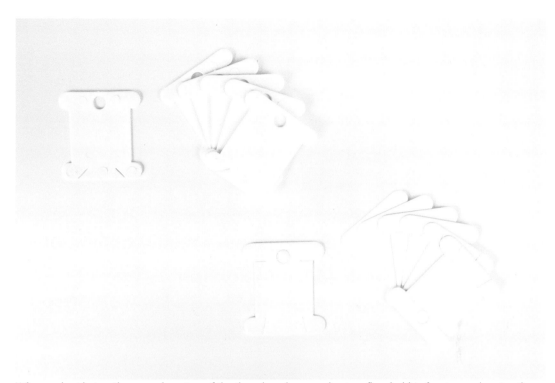

When embroidering, the unused portion of the thread can be wound onto a **floss bobbin** for storage, keeping the workspace tidy and not wasting thread. To distinguish thread colors, the floss bobbin can be labeled with the thread color number. The above is in plastic and the bottom is in paper.

The compartments in the **bobbin storage box** can neatly arrange the floss bobbins. Storage boxes come in various sizes and can be selected according to individual needs.

Excessively bright or dim light can cause eye discomfort or make it difficult to see the embroidery during long embroidery sessions. **Eye-protection lamps** have soft, bright light, making it more comfortable to work on your embroidery. It is important to choose an eye-protection lamp with white light, because yellow light can affect the judgement of thread colors.

3. Precautions to Note in Advance

This section mainly introduces the processing of the base fabric and the selection of embroidery thread. Paying attention to the relevant details can ensure that the embroidery is neater and the embroidery process is more efficient.

Processing the Base Fabric

Many fabrics are already cut with scissors when you purchase them. Although the edges may appear straight, they are often not aligned with the warp and

Cut an incision on the edge of the base fabric.

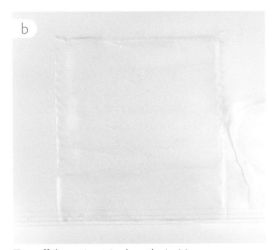

Tear off the entire strip along the incision.

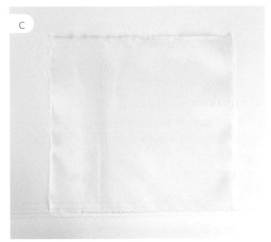

Adjust the base fabric on all four sides.

weft of the fabric and are slanted. Before use, adjustments and preparations should be made in terms of the four sides, size, cleanliness, and other factors.

Adjusting the sides of the base fabric. The recommended base fabric in this book is semi-transparent organza, a plain weave fabric with warp and weft lines interwoven. The simplest method for adjusting it is to cut a small incision in the fabric edge and tear off a narrow strip directly along the incision. By repeating this process for the remaining three sides, the processed base fabric will have four straight angles, and all four edges will be aligned with the warp and weft lines of the fabric. Whether it is for stretching or mounting, it will be very smooth and tidy (see steps a to c on page 34). Beginners can also use cotton as the base fabric, adjusting in the same way as organza.

Adjusting the size of the base fabric. When adjusting the size of the base fabric, the method of mounting the finished work should be considered first. Generally, the size of the mounting will be slightly larger than the embroidery area. In any case, when the size of the mounting is determined, the base fabric should be cut with at least an additional 3 cm on each side to facilitate the mounting process.

Ensuring the cleanliness of the base fabric. To ensure the final effect of the embroidery, it is best to avoid washing the embroidery after completion. Therefore, the selected base fabric should be clean. If there are stains on the base fabric, they should be cleaned first. Organza is an animal fiber, so a silk detergent or mild detergent should be used to wash it, and it should not be dehydrated. After cleaning, it can be rolled up with a towel with good water absorption to absorb the moisture until it is half-dry, and then laid flat on an ironing board to be ironed at medium temperature. Remember not to use high temperature. When ironing, the base fabric should be pulled straight and flattened, and the iron should move gently on the its surface, without pushing or pulling forcefully in a diagonal direction, which may cause the warp and weft lines of the material to be slanted.

Ironing the base fabric. If there are creases on the base fabric, they must be ironed flat before embroidery. Organza can be ironed at most at medium temperature (or the temperature between silk and wool). If stubborn creases cannot be ironed flat, spray water on them to wet the creases and then iron them at medium temperature until they are flat.

Selecting Thread

When taking thread, it is best to cut it to a length of about 30 cm. If the thread is too long, it is prone to knotting and fraying, which results in more time being required for each stitch. If the thread is too short, it will require frequent starting and ending of the thread and changing the thread, which is a waste of both time and thread.

Make sure that the color number of each thread is clear. If it is a bundle of threads, make sure that the color number ring is always present on the thread. If a piece of thread is wound on a floss bobbin, the color number should also be marked on the floss bobbin.

Ensure the Cleanliness of the Embroidery

Before starting embroidery, you should wash your hands to ensure that the embroidery thread and fabric are not contaminated. Sometimes, even a little sweat or oil on your hands can smudge the embroidery or fabric. If silk thread is used for embroidery, it is also important to take care of your hands. Any roughness on your hands may cause the silk thread to fray, affecting the uniformity and luster of the embroidery.

If an embroidery project takes a long time to complete, cover the embroidery with a clean, smooth cloth every day when you finish your embroidery work and leave the frame to prevent dust or dirt from falling on it.

Choosing an Embroidery Frame

The embroidery designs in this book come in two sizes: a square with a side length of 11 cm in Chapter Three and a circle with a diameter of 24 cm in Chapter Four.

For a 11 cm square design, it is recommended that you use an embroidery frame with a size of 18 cm, which will ensure that the round hoop does not press on the part of the design that is within the size of the mounting board. Organza is fragile, and the place where the hoop is tightly stretched may cause damage to the fabric, which should be avoided within the mounting range.

For a 24 cm circle design, it is recommended to use a scroll frame. Organza is not suitable for adjusting the position of the embroidery hoop, and the embroidery works in this book are relatively delicate. Adjusting the hoop to press on the already embroidered part may also damage the embroidery.

Ironing the Embroidery

When ironing the embroidery, avoid pressing the front of the embroidery directly with an iron. The marks of the heat erasable pen can be eliminated by blowing hot air from a hairdryer or steaming with an iron. Embroidery taken off a scroll frame generally does not need extra ironing, but embroidery taken off a hand-held frame needs to be ironed flat to remove the creases. When ironing, use a warm iron to iron the creased parts and then flatten them.

Avoid Sitting for Long Periods

When embroidering, be sure to avoid sitting for long periods of time without moving. You should stand up and move around every hour or so.

4. Preparation

This section introduces stretching and design transfer along with other preparations to be made before beginning the needlework.

Stretching

Stretching is a very important step in embroidery, and it is directly related to the success or failure of the piece. When stretching the base fabric, first pay attention to its direction of weave, then its tightness. The base fabric used in the examples in this book is organza, so only the key steps for stretching organza are explained.

Stretching method by using hoop rings. When embroidering a 11 cm square work, use an 18 cm embroidery hoop. If the bite force of embroidery hoop is not enough, wrapping the bandage around the inner ring can increase the friction. The steps for stretching the fabric onto the hoop are below.

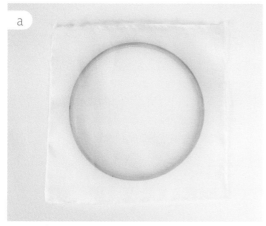

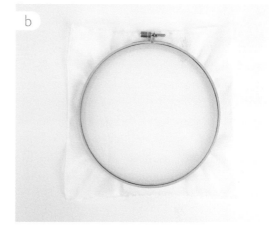

Loosen the screw to separate the inner and outer rings of the embroidery hoop, place the inner ring flat on the table, and place the flat base fabric of a suitable size and texture onto the inner ring. The ring should be in the center of the fabric.

Put the outer ring over the inner ring and clamp the fabric. Tighten the screw until the fabric can only be pulled slightly.

Slowly pull the fabric along the outer ring until the fabric is stretched taut, then tighten the screw. Note that when pulling the fabric, force should be applied evenly in each direction. Take care not to pull the fabric at an angle. To test the tightness of the base fabric, pat the surface with your hand. If it is tight enough, it will feel like the surface of a drum and produce a soft drumming sound. The organza is most likely to loosen near the hoop, where it is not easy to locate loose spots. Use your fingers to press along the edge of the hoop to find any slack spots and tighten them. When this is done, tighten the screw with a screwdriver to prevent the base fabric from becoming loose.

Stretching method by using scroll frame. The base fabric for an embroidery of 24 cm in diameter should be stretched using the scroll frame method. A scroll frame not only fits the fabric snugly, but also prevents wear when embroidering larger works. While embroidering, one hand works on top of the fabric and the other below it, which saves time. It takes several days to get used to embroidering on both sides of the fabric, but once you learn it, the work is much smoother. There is no fixed rule for which hand is on top of and which below the fabric. You can use whichever way is more comfortable for you. The steps for stretching are shown on pages 38 to 41.

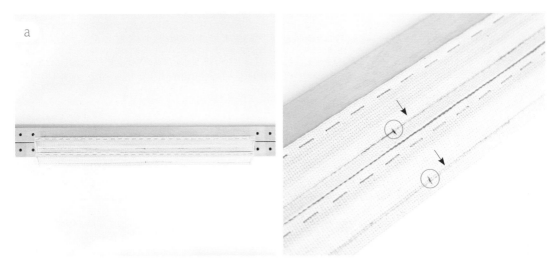

Place the two bars flat on the scroll frame, with the side with webbing facing up. If it is your first time using the scroll frame, begin by drawing a parallel line 1 cm from the edge of the webbing with an ink pen (see red arrows), and draw a short vertical line at the midpoint of the webbing as a marker (see green circles). You can use these marks for all future projects. Take care to confirm that the positions of the ribbons on the bars are the same and there is no misalignment. If they are misaligned, the center point of each bar should be measured and marked.

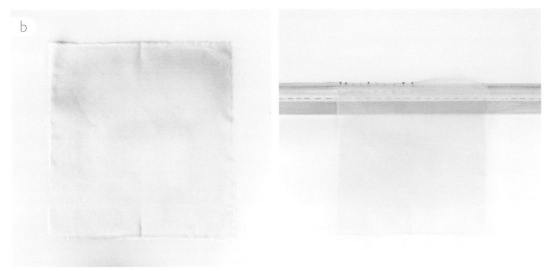

Cut the base fabric to size and tear it evenly, then fold it in half, left to right, press a small crease on the upper and lower ends of the fold, and unfold it, then align the upper crease to the mark on the webbing on the horizontal bar. Point and align the edge of this side of the base fabric with the edge of the webbing. Starting at the now aligned center point, use ball head pins to pin the sides, securing the fabric to the webbing.

If you are new to stretching, you can begin from the fixed center point, knot the double-strand cotton thread, and sew the base fabric to the webbing, from the center to one side, along the line you have drawn on the webbing. Ensure that the last stitch goes beyond the edge of the base fabric. The first and last stitch should be double stitched to prevent gaps or tearing. Use a straight stitch, about 0.5 cm apart. When one side has been sewn, sew the other side from the center point to the opposite end in the same way.

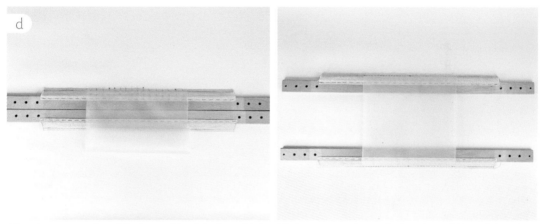

Align the center point of the lower side of the base fabric with the center point marked on the webbing of the other crossbar, and sew it in the same way.

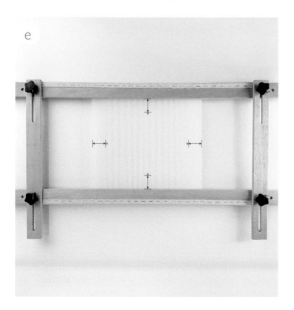

Turn the scroll frame over, place the drawing in the center of the base fabric, mark the top, bottom, left, and right side of the 24 cm circle with an erasable pen (as indicated by the four dots), then scroll the fabric, together with the webbing along the bar, to ensure that the top, bottom, left, and right sides of the 24 cm circle have a certain amount of space from the bar. Make sure that the fabric is taut and without wrinkles or skews as you roll it out. Insert the left and right vertical bars between the horizontal bars, stretch the fabric as straight as possible, and tighten the screws on the left and right vertical bars. Note that you can simply fix the fabric according to the left and right vertical axis as you stretch, continuing to tighten the screw first on one side, then the other two or three times. This will gradually stretch the base fabric until it is very tight. If you feel that pulling by hand does not make the fabric tight enough, you can use your crotch to support the vertical bar and tug the lower horizontal bar to tighten the material. At the same time, note that the upper and lower bars should be parallel to prevent stretching or marring of the base fabric.

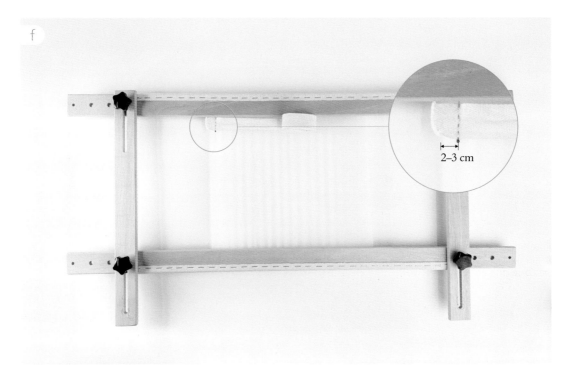

2–3 cm

After fixing the vertical axis, take an appropriate amount of webbing (I use a herringbone webbing) and fix it to one side of the base fabric with a ball pin. First ensure that the head of the webbing is perpendicular to the side of the base fabric. When fixing it, make sure to let the needle go through the webbing several times so that there are more supporting points within the width of the webbing.

Fold the webbing and pass it from above and below the vertical bar next to it and tighten the webbing so that the previously fixed fabric is taut. Then, tighten the part of the base fabric you are fixing in this step and fix it to the ribbon with a needle. The needle drop point should be moved 2 to 3 mm toward the center of the base fabric, compared to the previous fixed position, and the same method should then be used to fix the fabric.

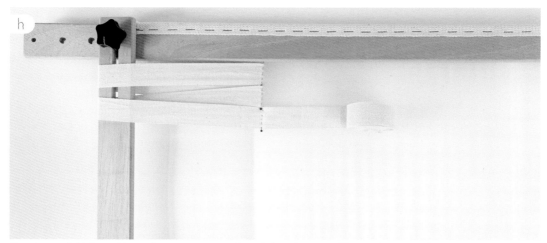

Continue to fold the webbing, this time passing it from below the vertical bar to above it, tightening the webbing and the corresponding base fabric again. Move the needle point the same way as in the previous step to fix it.

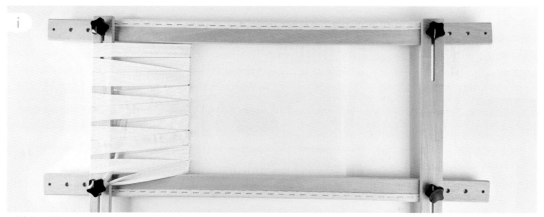

Fold the ribbon again and pass it from the top to the bottom of the vertical axis and continue to fix the fabric in the same way. Repeat this process until one side of the fabric is fully set. Each fixing progresses 2 to 3 mm at a time to ensure that the fabric is stretched taut. Finally, the remaining part of the webbing is tightened and knotted diagonally to the horizontal and vertical bars, and the excess webbing can be tucked into the slanted piece of the stretched webbing.

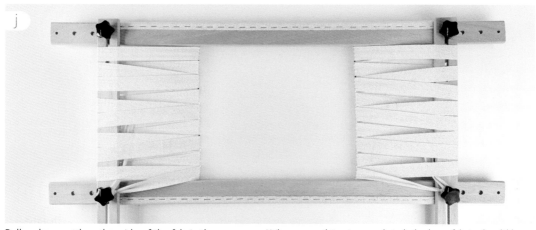

Pull and secure the other side of the fabric the same way. When everything is completed, the base fabric should be very flat and taut. If it feels loose when pressed, you should adjust the tightness of the webbing and the distance between the upper and lower bars. Base fabric that is not stretched tightly enough will ruin the embroidery.

Pattern Transfer

If the pattern is transferred before the base fabric is stretched, the stretching process will likely distort the pattern, so the correct method is to apply the pattern after stretching. The steps for transferring the pattern to the organza are laid out below.

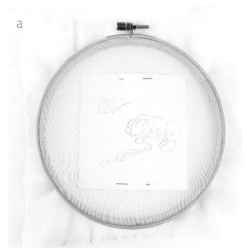

a

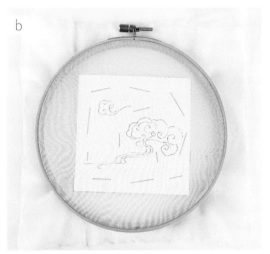

b

Secure the pattern to the fabric. Because the organza is thin and almost translucent, the pattern can be easily traced without additional lighting. Copy the pattern on the gatefold at the end of the book in its original size, trimming off as much excess paper as possible so that the drawing is smaller than the frame. Pin the cut-out pattern to the base fabric, paying close attention to the upper, lower, left, and right directions of the fabric and the cut-out pattern.

Fix the pattern by basting it to the fabric with any cotton or embroidery thread. Basting uses a straight stitch with relatively long stitches. The size can be between 1 and 3 cm, depending on the size of the drawing. Be careful not to let the stitches cross the lines of the pattern, so as to avoid inconvenience later.

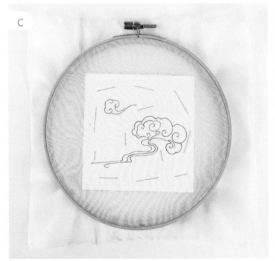

c

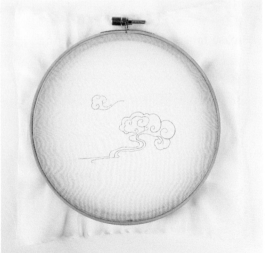

When tracing, place the hoop or scroll frame on the table. Because the frame itself has some depth, the fabric will not touch the tabletop, making it hard for you to apply force when tracing, so it is advisable to place a flat, hard object below the fabric while tracing. Though the traditional Chinese drawing method which uses a brush dipped in light ink is still used today, for beginners, it is more convenient to use a heat or water erasable pen, making it easier to make corrections and to eliminate excess traces when the embroidery is completed. The image on the right shows the effect of removing threads and pattern.

Starting and Ending of Embroidery

Chinese embroidery does not usually use knots to start and end threads. On the one hand, knots can affect the appearance, especially for double-sided embroidery, which should be identical on both sides and look neat and tidy. It is essential to use a hidden thread technique. When using scroll frames for large-sized embroidery works, it would be cumbersome to knot every time you start or end the thread because you need to flip over the scroll frame. To hide the loose ends, put a few tiny short stitches in an unnoticeable place to secure the thread at the beginning and end of each thread, called a starting stitch. However, for beginners, it is recommended to start and end the stitches with a knot. However, it should be noted that if a transparent base fabric is used, the knotted threads need to be hidden where they are covered by the embroidery.

Starting stitch technique. The starting stitch involves putting two or three adjacent tiny short stitches near the position where the first stitch exits, and then trimming the excess thread against the base fabric. Note that these stitches

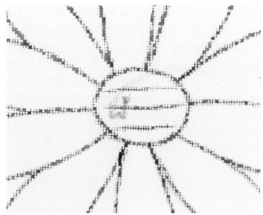

Fig. 44   Starting stitch.

Fig. 45   The starting stitch ends in blank space.

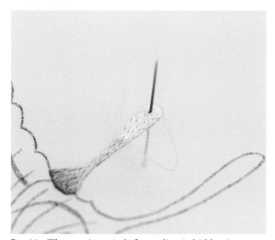

Fig. 46   The starting stitch for ending is hidden in the embroidery, with the needle taken out of the gap between the two threads.

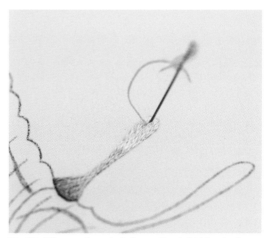

Fig. 47   The starting stitch for ending is hidden in the embroidery, with the needle entering through the gap again.

should not exceed 1 mm. The smaller the stitches, the better the fixing effect on the thread.

Starting stitch position. The starting stitch must be made in a location that will be covered by the embroidery thread. The starting stitch is generally made inside the pattern that is about to be embroidered, close to the first stitch's exit point (see fig. 44 on page 43). The starting stitch for ending, which is also called finishing stitch, can be made near the last stitch, but it should also be covered by the embroidery (see fig. 45 on page 43). If there is no blank area left for the last stitch, you need to hide the stitch in a location where you have already embroidered. The specific method is to take the needle out of the gap between the two threads, and then enter the needle through this gap again (see figs. 46 and 47 on page 43). The stitches should be very short. Two or three short stitches do not need to be taken out of the same gap, just close together.

Prepare Practice Materials

Prepare a hoop and stretch the same base fabric as the work you are about to do for some practice. What needs to be practiced mainly includes:

Adapting to the fiber characteristics of the base fabric. Each different base fabric's warp and weft thickness and weave density will require stitching with different needle densities when embroidering the shape's contour. You need to adapt in advance.

Stitching technique practice. When learning a new stitching technique, practice on the cloth until you can operate it correctly and achieve the desired effect.

Partial practice. When embroidering shapes with corners or complicated stitch combinations, you can practice on the test fabric first and then embroider on the base fabric when you are confident. This will avoid repeated removals that can damage the base fabric, affecting the final embroidery effect.

Learning to Analyze Embroidery Objects

For beginners, it is recommended to use a pencil to draw the direction of the stitch lines on the pattern first. If you can draw a smooth line pattern with a pencil, it will be much easier to embroider. The success of embroidery depends on whether the silk threads are arranged properly. Before embroidering, observe the subject and carefully interpret the silk grain direction and the length of stitches from a demonstration sample for better efficiency in the embroidery process.

When you have gained a better perspective on the correct silk grain direction, use water-erasable or heat-erasable pens to draw auxiliary lines indicating the turns of the silk grain within the shape to prevent issues such as confusion in thread direction or uneven transitions during embroidery.

Some Technical Terms

1. **Base fabric:** The fabric used as the foundation for embroidery.
2. **Needle in and needle out:** During the embroidery process, when the needle pierces the fabric from underneath and goes up, it is called an "needle out." When the needle pierces the fabric from above and goes down, it is called a "needle in." In describing the stitching technique, we often use the expression "1 out, 2 in," which refers to the first stitch coming up from underneath and the second stitch going down from above.
3. **Stitch:** When stitching, every two stitches (one needle in and one needle out) will create a line, which is called a "stitch." The length of this line is called the stitch length, also known as stitch spacing. In the chain stitch technique, the stitch length (or stitch spacing) refers to the distance between the tail and the top of a U-shaped loop.
4. **Waterway:** In decorative patterns such as flower petals, to distinguish between shapes with similar colors and increase the decorative effect of the pattern, a gap is left at the intersection of two adjacent patterns, which is the width of one embroidery thread. This gap is called a "waterway." The waterway should be left parallel and uniform, and both edges should be stitched neatly and smoothly to make the embroidered product have a clear and beautiful outline. The waterway should be drawn when creating a pattern.
5. **Overlapping:** At the intersection of embroidered patterns, without leaving a waterway, the upper shape is pressed onto the edge of the lower shape, which is called "overlapping." When doing this, the lower shape should be stitched first, and the stitch length should go slightly beyond the drawn border. Then the upper shape is stitched, and its edge should cover the edge of the lower shape. The edge of the upper shape must be stitched accurately and smoothly to make the pattern exquisite and beautiful.
6. **Silk grain direction or stitch direction:** The silk grain direction refers to the direction of the embroidery thread arrangement. Most of the embroidery patterns are completed by stitches of straight lines, such as satin stitch, long and short stitch, and shaded satin stitch. However, the objects embroidered, whether they are flowers, leaves, animals, people, clouds, or flowing water, all have twisting and turning postures. When embroidering, a row of stitches needs to be interlaced and combined to form a smooth, flowing effect that matches the object being portrayed, in order to portray the twisting and turning of plants, the direction of animal hair growth, and the movement of clouds and water with meticulous detail. The stitching technique of embroidery is easy to learn and master, but the application and combination of stitching techniques is the most important skill in embroidery.

CHAPTER THREE
Embroidery Stitches

This chapter explains sixteen types of needlework techniques in traditional Chinese embroidery. Each needlework technique includes step-by-step diagrams and a detailed illustration of the corresponding small embroidery piece. When learning these sixteen techniques, there are some recommended sequences, such as for the techniques related to lines, which include chain stitch, backstitch, stem stitch, and slanted stem stitch. Among these, it is recommended that embroiderers learn slanted stem stitch after mastering stem stitch. For techniques related to surfaces, it is best to first learn satin stitch, then proceed to learn basic encroaching satin stitch and encroaching satin stitch with hidden threads. Finally, it is best to follow the sequence of learning regular shaded satin stitch first, then learning round shaded satin stitch, long and short shaded satin stitch, long and short stitch, and padded satin stitch. Knot stitch and bead embroidery can be learned separately, but because the corresponding embroidery pieces involve satin stitch, long and short stitch, and slanted stem stitch techniques, it is advisable to practice these techniques before working on the corresponding embroidery projects.

The actual sized paper pattern of each embroidery project can be found in the gatefold at the end of the book.

The brands of embroidery threads used for the projects are listed in the Materials part and only color numbers are written in the text of the step instructions.

Fig. 48 The projects of *Plum Blossoms* (see page 99), *Camellia* (see page 85), and *Daisy* (see page 74).

1. Chain Stitch

With a history of more than 3,000 years in China, chain stitch is a very ancient technique (fig. 49). During the thousand years spanning from the Western Zhou dynasty to the Tang dynasty, chain stitch has always been the most popular embroidery stitch, and it has been passed down until today. It is widely used in embroidery work each day. The chain stitch is suitable for expressing lines and monochromatic block surfaces which are not only decorative but also resistant to wear and able to protect the fabric.

Fig. 49 Embroidery with Cloud Pattern of Western Han Dynasty (206 BC–AD 25)
Hunan Provincial Museum
The various types of embroidery patterns evolved from cloud patterns during the Han dynasty were all embroidered with silk embroidery thread using the chain stitch method, reflecting the unique poetic style of the Han dynasty and the luxury of its aristocratic life.

Embroidery Technique

1

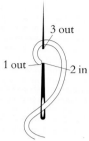

Starting the stitch: The first stitch comes out from the starting point of the pattern, and the second stitch enters near the first stitch so that the thread forms a circle on the fabric. The third stitch is about 2–3 mm in front of the first stitch, and the loop is tightened to form a full drop shape. Note that the distance between the first and third stitches can be reduced or enlarged according to the pattern and the thickness of the thread used.

2

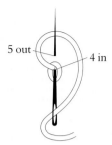

The fourth stitch enters near the side of the third stitch. Make the thread form a circle on the surface of the cloth. The fifth stitch should exit from about 2–3 mm in front of the third stitch and tighten the loop to a full drop shape.

3

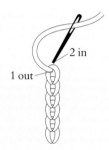

Ending: Following steps 1 and 2, the loops formed each time are roughly the same. At the end of the embroidery, the position of the first stitch is on the same vertical line as that of the third and fifth stitches in steps 1 and 2. Tighten the loops so that the size of each loop is basically the same. Insert the second stitch next to the edge of the loop.

4

The image shows the finished effect of the embroidery.

Tips

1. When embroidering, pay attention to the uniformity of the stitches, moderate the length, and control the force with which you pull the thread. If it is too lax, the loop will be loose, and if it is too forceful, the loop will be too tight.
2. The coils on the surface of the cloth should be consistent in size, full, and beautiful.
3. Generally, the thicker the thread, the bigger the stitch, and the thinner the thread, the smaller the stitch should be.
4. When coiling the block surface with chain stitch, be careful not to leave unsightly gaps between rows. At sharp corners, shorter stitches should be used to create smooth curves.

Embroidery Project: *The* Peng *Bird*

This work absorbs and integrates the cloud pattern and flying bird elements in the embroidery of Han dynasty. The design depicts a *peng* bird soaring, riding on the clouds, as stated in the Chinese ancient philosophy classic *Zhuangzi—Wandering at Will*: "The *peng* bird migrates to the South China Sea, beating the water and stirring up waves over three thousand *li*; riding the wind and circling upward, he soars to a height of ninety thousand *li*." It is a romantic, unrestrained image.

Materials

Base fabric: white organza.
Embroidery threads: **OLYMPUS** No. 25 embroidery threads 190# and 556# (single strand).

Steps

Transfer the pattern to the base fabric with a heat erasable pen. Using 190# red single-strand embroidery thread, start with 2–3 small stitches near the tip of the pattern (position 1). This will be covered by embroidery thread later in the work.

Using the chain stitch method, start to embroider along the contour line from position 1, ending at position 2, where the stitches are ended.

Beginning at position 2, extend along the contour line with a new chain stitch line to position 3 and end the stitch. Note that the starting position of the stitches should be staggered from the last stitch of position 2, so that the tip of position 2 remains sharp and, at the same time, the new stitch can connects to the earlier stitch naturally.

Starting from position 3, use the chain stitch method to embroider along the outline until the stitch is end at position 1. Refer to step 3 for points requiring attention at the starting and ending positions.

6

Using chain stitch method to embroider from position 1 to the inside of the outermost line, begin another row. Take note that a) the embroidery should be close to the inner side of the outer contour line, b) you should embroider in the same direction as the outer circle, and c) the chain stitch line of this circle is not continuous and can be interrupted according to the needs of the specific piece, just like the outer circle. Start the next stitch at a suitable position to continue the pattern.

Use the same method to fill the rest of the blank space with chain stitch. Note that when the remaining block inside the pattern is small and irregular in shape, the lines of chain stitch can be flexibly interrupted and the stitching can be restarted at a suitable position, but take note that the direction of the needlework should be as consistent as possible with the outer embroidery. At the end, make 2–3 small stitches with the excess thread in the gaps inside the pattern, where they will not be visible, then cut off any excess thread.

7

With 190# thread, start stitching from position 4, using chain stitch method along the contour line to complete a smooth, continuous contour line. Refer to step 3 for the treatment of sharp corners in this stage of the work.

Starting from position 5, embroider along the contour line with chain stitch method. Complete the embroidery along the contour line, ending at position 5.

Fill the inside of the pattern with chain stitch method. Refer to steps 5 and 6 for the specific technique.

Using 556# yellow single-strand embroidery thread, start stitching from position 6. End the stitching at position 7.

Embroider three circles with 190# red single-strand embroidery thread. A single circle is embroidered from the outline. When the ends meet, there is no need to end the stitch. It can just be coiled inward until the center is filled.

Use 556# yellow single-strand embroidery thread, start from position 8 and embroider to position 9. Then, start from position 10 and embroidery to position 11. See step 3 for the technique to be used on sharp angles.

Again, use 556# yellow single-strand embroidery thread, start from position 11 and embroider to position 8, completing the yellow section of the contour embroidery.

Fill the inside of the pattern with chain stitch method. For details of technique, see steps 6 and 7.

2. Stem Stitch

The stem stitch has been used in China since the Tang dynasty, with a history of about 1,500 years (fig. 50). The lines embroidered using stem stitch are continuous, compact, and smooth, without revealing the stitch marks. It is still the most commonly used stitching technique for straight lines, curves, and outlines today.

Fig. 50 Statue of Manjushri (partial view of the *Lingjiushan Mountain Discourse of Shakyamuni Buddha* painting)

The British Museum

The eyebrow, eyelash, and eye contours of the Buddha image were found to be embroidered using stem stitch technique. This embroidery of Tang dynasty Buddha statue was discovered in the Thousands Buddha Cave at Dunhuang, China. The lines on the embroidery are drawn as if with a single stroke, without revealing any stitches, and they are uniformly thick and neat.

Embroidery Technique

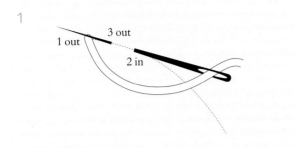

1

Starting the stitch: The first stitch is made by bringing the needle out from the starting point of the pattern. The second stitch is made approximately 3 mm away from the first stitch, taking care not to pull the thread on the fabric too tightly. Leave some thread to be held with the left hand. The third stitch is made by bringing the needle out at the midpoint between the first and second stitches. At this point, the thread held by the left hand should be positioned below the embroidery needle. Slowly tighten the thread with the right hand while pulling it slightly in the opposite direction. This step ensures that the embroidery thread on the fabric is tightened and closely adheres to the fabric.

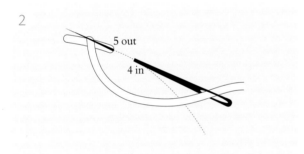

2

The fourth stitch starts from the endpoint of the third stitch and advances approximately 3 mm forward. Again, leave a portion of the thread without pulling it tight, holding it with the left hand. The fifth stitch is made by bringing the needle out from the same stitch hole as the second stitch, with the thread held by the left hand still positioned below the embroidery needle. Slowly tighten the thread with the right hand while pulling it firmly in the opposite direction.

3

The stem stitch is completed.

Tips

1. The stitch length for the stem stitch is not fixed. When embroidering straight lines and gentle curves, the stitch length can be around 3–4 mm. However, when encountering sharp turns in the lines, the stitch length should be reduced accordingly to create smooth curves. It is important to maintain even stitches while embroidering.

2. Generally, thicker threads produce larger stitch length, while finer threads produce smaller stitch length.

3. When embroidering with the stem stitch, remember to pull the thread in the opposite direction of the embroidery line to tighten the thread.

4. The segment of thread held by the left hand should always be on one side of the needle, i.e., below or above the embroidery needle, to help create continuous lines that twist like a spiral. If this segment of thread keeps switching above and below, the continuity of the line may be broken.

Embroidery Project: *Auspicious Clouds*

In ancient Chinese mythology and legends, the colorful clouds ridden by immortals symbolize auspiciousness and happiness. The design of this artwork draws inspiration from the cloud patterns in traditional Chinese culture, which are associated with good fortune. The design has a graceful, flowing appearance.

Materials
Base fabric: white organza.
Embroidery threads: **DMC** No. 25 embroidery thread 4022# (single strand).

Steps

Trace the embroidery design onto the fabric using a heat erasable pen.

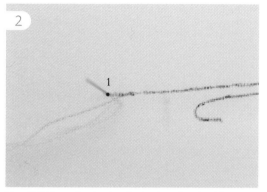

Use 4022# gradient color single-strand embroidery thread. Begin stitching the tail end of the cloud with a thread length at least four times the length of the segment to be embroidered. Start with two small short stitches, positioning the short stitch close to position 1 near the tip of the pattern. Make sure to accurately stitch along the line drawn in step 1 to ensure that the stitches cover the line. Keep the two short stitches slightly apart, avoiding the needle entry points of the first few stitches in the subsequent stitching process.

The first stitch begins at the starting point, the second stitch crosses 3 mm to the right, and the third stitch starts halfway between the first two stitches, with the thread (or the loop) on the fabric surface positioned below the needle.

The fourth stitch enters the fabric 3 mm away from the exit point of the third stitch. The fifth stitch exits from the entry hole of the second stitch. At this point, the thread or the loop on the fabric remains below the embroidery needle. Repeat steps 3 and 4.

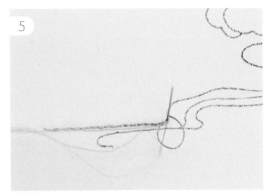

When turning the line, shorten the stitch length to create smooth curves at the turn.

After completing the entire line, following the traced line, make two small short stitches closely to secure and finish the thread.

Following steps 2–6, embroider the second curved line. When finishing the second curved line, if there are no adjacent lines to make short stitches along, you can hide the short stitches underneath the embroidered lines. Alternatively, you can use the method described in steps 11–14 on page 57 to finish the line.

There should be no gaps at the junction between the second and third curved lines. When making the first stitch of the third curved line, it is best to exit the needle from the gap between the embroidered thread of the second curved line and the fabric surface. This will create a smoother, tighter junction.

When encountering inward-pointing acute angles as shown in the diagram, you can enter the needle at position 1 (the vertex of the angle), skip to position 2 to make a small short stitch, then return to position 1 for an exit stitch and continue with the stem stitch. This technique will result in a sharp, clean angle.

Complete the entire curved line using the same method.

11

Flip the fabric to the reverse side, and you will see a curved line composed of connected short segments. Insert the needle from left to right below the nearest segment, being careful not to go through to the front side of the fabric. Pull the thread tight.

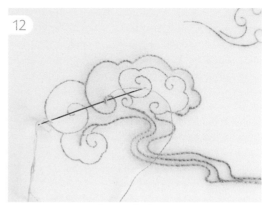

12

Continue inserting the needle from left to right below the next segment, pulling the thread tight as you go.

13

Always insert the needle from left to right and repeat this step for 4–5 times.

14

After pulling the thread tight, trim off the excess thread along the fabric surface. You can also use steps 11–14 for starting, with the difference being that for starting, you should leave a 5–8 cm thread end below the fabric before stitching as usual until completing the entire line. Then, insert the remaining 5–8 cm thread end into the embroidery needle and finish the stitch using the same method.

15

Complete the entire design using the same method.

Note: If you run out of thread and cannot complete the entire line, you can make two short stitches to finish the thread. Then, take another thread of the same color, and continue stitching from the end point of the previous thread. Again, make two short stitches to start, and exit from the entry hole of the second-to-last stitch of the previous thread, ensuring a seamless connection. However, excessive starting and finishing short stitches may inconvenience the embroidery process, so as much as possible, it is best to avoid changing thread during embroidery.

3. Slanted Stem Stitch

The slanted stem stitch appears in various decorative Song dynasty embroidery works (fig. 51). This stitching technique allows for more flexibility in the variation of lines, such as those used to depict finer plant stems, leaf veins, folds in clothing, and outlines with varying thickness.

The slanted stem stitch is a technique that falls between the satin stitch and the stem stitch. The satin stitch can represent broader areas, while the stem stitch is limited to fine lines with a constant width. The slanted stem stitch incorporates the

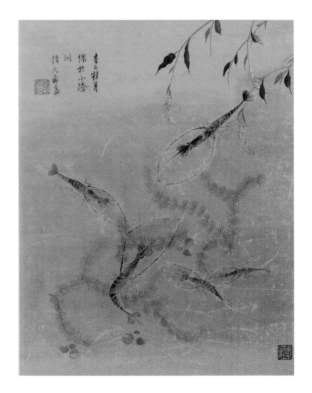

Fig. 51 *Grass Shrimp*
This is a piece by the famous embroiderer Han Ximeng. The water plants floating in the background and winding into graceful lines are represented using the slanted stem stitch technique.

silk grain direction of the satin stitch into the expression of the lines, which allows for the flexible handling of embroidery, enabling smooth transitions from thin to thick or continuously changing thickness in the lines. The use of the slanted stem stitch in ancient Chinese embroidery marked a new level of expressiveness in line representation.

Embroidery Technique

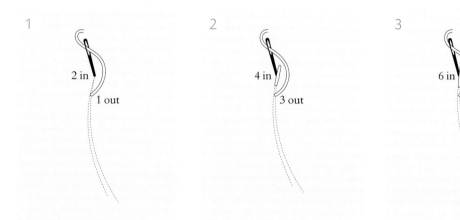

As shown in the diagram, the first stitch follows the right outline of the pattern, coming out approximately 3 mm from the tip. The second stitch is inserted at the pattern's tip.

The third stitch follows the right outline of the pattern, exiting approximately 1.5 mm down from the end point of the first stitch. The fourth stitch begins at the midpoint of the left side of the first stitch. When inserting the needle, angle it slightly to the right, allowing the point to hide slightly beneath the first stitch.

The fifth stitch follows the right outline of the pattern, exiting approximately 1.5 mm down from the end point of the third stitch. The sixth stitch begins at the midpoint of the left side of the second stitch, which is to the left of the exit point of the first stitch. When inserting the needle, angle it slightly to the right, allowing the point to hide slightly beneath the second stitch.

Repeat the above steps, continuously stitching along the outline as you move downward. As the pattern gradually transitions from thin to thick, the direction of the stitches will also change from vertical to gradually slanted. As shown in the diagram, the exit points on the right side of the outline gradually decrease the spacing as the pattern becomes thicker. Similarly, the entry points on the left side also gradually decrease the spacing.

By arranging the direction and density of stitches based on the pattern's thickness variations, you can easily control the changes in the thickness of the embroidered lines, allowing for precise control and flexibility in creating patterns with varying thickness.

1. The length of stitches using the slanted stem stitch technique should be adjusted according to the width and intricacies of the pattern. The mention of 3 mm of Embroidery Technique step 1 on page 59 was meant to make the process easier for beginners. In practice, experienced embroiderers will adapt the stitch length and handle the transitions more flexibly to suit the specific needs of the design.
2. Compared to the stem stitch technique, once proficient, using the slanted stem stitch is simpler and faster, making it more efficient than the stem stitch method. However, becoming skilled in using the slanted stem stitch requires much practice and training.
3. In the slanted stem stitch technique, each stitch's entry should be slightly slanted below the center of the previous stitch to appropriately hide the needle point.
4. The slanted stem stitch technique can be used in two ways: Following the above steps, bring the needle out from the left outline and bring it in from the right outline; or exit the needle from the right outline and enter it from the left outline. You can try a few times to find the method you are most comfortable with.

Embroidery Project: *Aquatic Plants*

Here, we will use the aquatic plants from the work *Grass Shrimp* on page 58 as a reference for the demo of the slanted stem stitch technique.

Materials
Base fabric: white organza.
Embroidery threads: **DMC** No. 25 embroidery threads 4050#, 4045# and 4047# (single strand).

Steps

Draw the embroidery design on the base fabric using a heat erasable pen. Since this design mainly emphasizes lines, pay attention to depicting the varying thickness of the lines while drawing. Start the embroidery from the part marked with a star as shown in the diagram.

Embroider the fine leaves of the seaweed starting from the point indicated in the diagram, using a single strand of 4050# embroidery thread. First, make a starting stitch on the fine leaves of the seaweed to be embroidered.

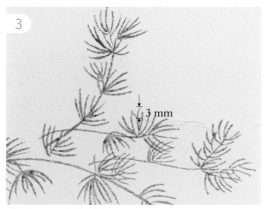

The first stitch should begin at a position approximately 3 mm to the left of the tip of the fine leaf.

The second stitch should be inserted at the tip of this fine leaf.

For the third stitch on the left image, bring the needle down (toward the root of the fine leaf) approximately 1.5 mm from where the first stitch emerged.

For the fourth stitch on the right image, insert the needle at the midpoint between the embroidered line created by the first and second stitches. You can either insert the needle from the left side or the right side of the line. When inserting the needle, slightly tilt the needle tip toward the direction of the line. Pierce through from the underside of the already embroidered thread to create an effect where one thread holds down the other thread. The diagram of this project shows all stitching starting from the left side. It is important to note that the specific direction can be determined based on the embroiderer's preference and what feels more comfortable while stitching. Once the direction of stitching is decided, it should be consistently maintained throughout.

The fifth stitch should come down (toward the root of the fine leaf) approximately 1.5 mm from the third stitch.

The sixth stitch starts halfway between the thread tracks of the third and fourth stitches. It enters from the left side and is almost level with the exit point of the first stitch, at one thread's distance apart. When inserting the needle, tilt the needle slightly in the direction of the thread tracks and pierce it from the underside of the previously embroidered thread.

8

Following the same steps, continue stitching until you reach the root of this fine leaf. Once you finish the embroidery, the stitches should be spaced evenly and the curve should have a natural arc.

9

Bring the embroidery thread from the back to the bottom of fine leaf on the right and make a small short stitch there. This way, the thread at the back will not be visible due to horizontal tension. If you are using an opaque base fabric, there is no need to make the small stitch. You can directly embroider the next section of the thin leaf.

10

The first stitch should come out approximately 3 mm away from the tip of the leaf, and the second stitch should enter at the tip. Please note that when embroidering specific objects, if the shape of the tip is very curved, you should adjust and shorten the distance between the exit point and the tip accordingly to ensure that the embroidered lines adhere to the shape of the curve.

11

The third stitch should come down approximately 1.5 mm from the first stitch, toward the bottom of the fine leaf. The fourth stitch starts halfway between the thread track of the first and second stitches. As with the previous fine leaf, it enters from the left side of the thread track with the needle slightly tilted in the direction of the thread track when inserting it from the underside of the previously embroidered thread.

The embroidery method for the sixth and seventh stitches is the same as before.

Complete the embroidery of the second fine leaf.

The third leaf is relatively long. When pulling the embroidery thread from the back to the front for stitching, you will need to make two short stitches at the base and lower part to ensure that the thread at the back is not visible. After making the short stitches, continue the embroidery using the previous method.

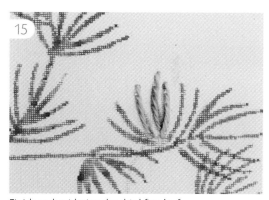

Finish embroidering the third fine leaf.

The fourth fine leaf is slightly thicker than the previous ones. After stitching the first and second stitches, the exit point of the third stitch is closer to the first stitch, approximately 1 mm. Similarly, the entry point of the fourth stitch is closer to the second stitch.

Shorten the distance between the following stitches and the previous stitches to ensure thicker lines when embroidering.

According to the thickness of the fine leaves, choose the density of the stitch spacing. Finish embroidering the first group of aquatic plant fine leaves.

Pull the embroidery thread at the back of the fabric with short stitches to the next starting point and begin embroidering from there.

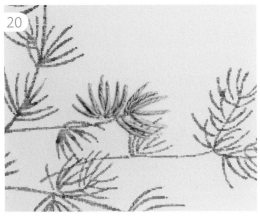

Using the same method, complete the embroidery of the second group of leaves.

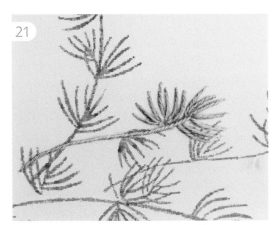

To embroider the branch of this group of leaves, use the same method as the first step, embroidering them in the same way as the first fine leaf since the branch is thin and doesn't have any variations in thickness.

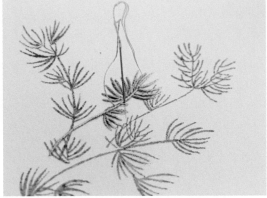

When encountering the need to cross over already embroidered branches or leaves, follow the normal stitch spacing and embroider over the existing embroidery thread. Depending on the specific situation, you can either stitch over the existing thread if it's feasible, or if necessary, you can insert or pull out the needle on the existing embroidery thread.

Complete the overlapping stitched lines.

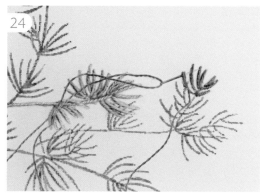

Use a single strand of 4045# embroidery thread and embroider the rightmost cluster of aquatic plants using the slanted stem stitch. The shape of the leaf shown in the diagram is quite unique, with a wider top. After stitching the first, second, and third stitches with normal entry and exit points, the fourth stitch's entry point can be aligned with the first stitch, directly adjacent to its left side.

Embroider the following stitches with normal spacing as usual.

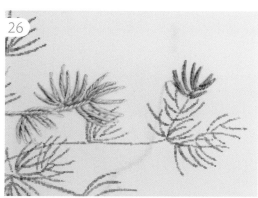

The completed effect. Subtle variations in the shape of the leaves can make the artwork more vivid. Different forms of leaves and branches can also help beginners better understand and master the various changes while using the slanted stem stitch.

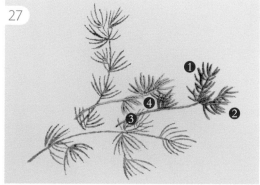

Embroider this group of aquatic plants in the order of 1, 2, 3, and 4 as shown in the diagram, with 3 referring to the branch.

Using a single strand of 4047# embroidery thread, embroider the aquatic plant as shown in the diagram. Start by stitching the leaf section first using the slanted stem stitch.

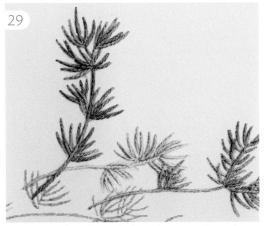

29

Continue embroidering the branch section. Since this branch is thicker, you should slightly shorten the stitch spacing and adjust the angle of the stitches accordingly.

30

Use a single strand of 4045# embroidery thread to embroider the fine leaves at positions 1 and 2 as shown in the diagram.

31

Using a single strand of 4047# embroidery thread, embroider the largest aquatic plant at the bottom starting from the front end (rightmost side) using the slanted stem stitch. Follow the sequence as shown in the diagram to complete the embroidery.

4. Backstitch

The use of backstitch in China dates back at least to the Yuan dynasty (1279–1368), making it over 600 years old (fig. 52). Backstitch has a series of stitches that are connected and can create intricate lines like stem stitch (see page 53), but the stitches of backstitch are visibly distinct and can't be hidden like the stem stitch.

During the Qing dynasty, the embroidery artist Shen Shou mentioned that the stitch length of high-quality embroidery created with backstitch should be "three stitches

in the length of one sesame seed." This means that three consecutive stitches should add up to approximately the length of a sesame seed (i.e., each stitch is less than 1 mm). A well-crafted backstitch embroidery creates a grainy effect with each stitch, especially if it is crafted with silk thread, making it appear like tiny, crystal pearls that are highly decorative.

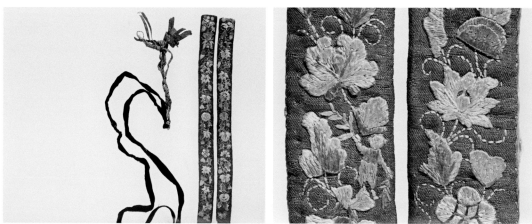

Fig. 52 A Lake Blue Dark Flower Silk Belt Embroidered with Children Playing with Flowers Pattern
The Ethnicity Museum in Longhua, Hebei Province
Many clothing and textiles from the Yuan dynasty have been unearthed in Hebei Province in China. Some of the embroidery on these textiles show the clear use of backstitch. The picture shows an embroidered belt used by women to tie their robes. The smooth, curled flower vines seen in the details were embroidered using the backstitch technique.

Embroidery Technique

1

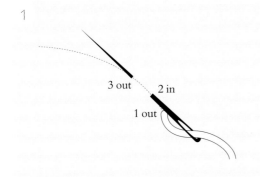

Starting the stitch: Pulling the needle up from the starting point of the pattern. Second stitch: Cross over an appropriate distance and insert the needle. Third stitch: Move forward and insert the needle equal distance between the first and second stitches.

2

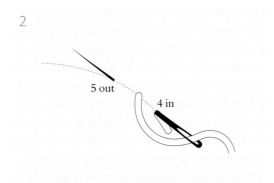

Fourth stitch: Go back to the second stitch and insert the needle. Fifth stitch: Cross over the same distance as before and take the needle out. It is important to insert the fourth stitch into the same hole as the second stitch to ensure continuity and tightness of the embroidery.

3

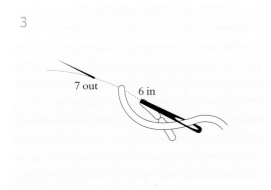

The sixth and seventh stitches are the same as the fourth and fifth stitches, and this process is repeated.

4

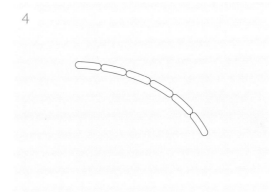

This is the finished effect of the backstitch.

Tips

1. The stitch length of the backstitch should be as uniform as possible. If there is a turn, the stitch length should be adjusted accordingly to ensure that the curve is smooth.
2. The stitch length should not be too large or the line will appear weak and limp. If you want to increase the stitch length, you can use a thicker embroidery thread to create a fuller visual effect.
3. The stitch length of the backstitch is smaller than that of the stem stitch. The thread end can be secured as described on page 57. For the beginning of the embroidery, the small short stitches can be hidden using a starting stitch technique in the next embroidery area, as long as it does not affect the stitching process.

Embroidery Project: *Water Waves*

As early as the Neolithic period, pottery with beautiful swirling water patterns appeared in China's Yellow River basin. The philosopher Laozi once said, "The highest good is like water" (meaning that the characteristics of the greatest virtues are like water), which illustrates the Chinese people's fondness for and unique understanding of water, which has penetrated Chinese culture. The pattern of this work is inspired by a traditional Chinese water pattern design, using gradient embroidery thread colors to highlight the lively, light nature of water.

Materials

Base fabric: white organza.
Embroidery threads: **DMC** No. 25 embroidery thread 4220# (single strand).

Steps

Trace the embroidery pattern onto the base fabric using a heat erasable pen.

Prepare about 60 cm of embroidery thread for stitching. Use 2 small short stitches to start stitching near the tip of the pattern (dot 1) and position it accurately along the line drawn in step 1. Be sure to keep the two short stitches slightly apart and to avoid the drop point for formal embroidery.

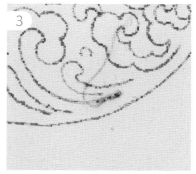

Using backstitch technique, stitch from the beginning of the line, controlling the stitch length at around 1 mm, and keeping the stitch marks as even as possible.

the loop under the base fabric

This work uses organza as a base fabric, which is very transparent. It is necessary to hide the embroidery thread on the back of the base fabric as much as possible to keep it from affecting the front image. Especially when encountering sharp corners or some slightly raised curves as shown by the green dot in the figure, you should use your left hand to draw the loop under the base fabric to the side of the pattern that is raised, then drop the needle, and then tighten the thread. This way, the thread at the backside of the fabric will line up with the pattern's thread and not be visible from the front. The backstitch is a reverse stitch, so you need to use force in the opposite direction to tighten the thread.

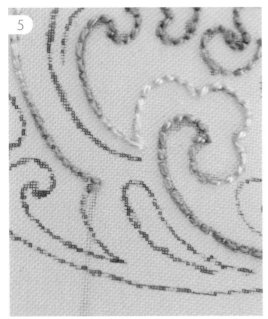

The thread at the backside of the fabric will be hidden after completing the entire stitch in this way.

For best result after finishing the whole line, you can change the thread at any time during the embroidery process. Just follow the method mentioned in the technique of stem stitch to end the thread (steps 11–14 on page 57), and then take another thread to continue stitching. However, please pay attention to the transition of the gradation of colors.

After finishing a continuous curve, make two starting stitches at the beginning of the next line segment to continue stitching.

Complete the embroidery of this section of the line.

Continue embroidery using the same method.

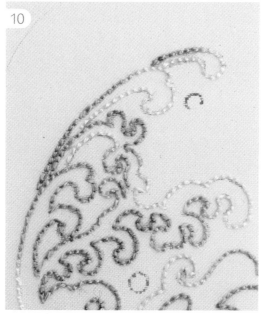

Continue embroidering using the same method. Pay attention to the waves in the upper left corner of the pattern; the colors used should resemble the demonstration piece as much as possible in order to achieve a light, graceful effect. You can experiment with color selection to accurately control the desired color combination.

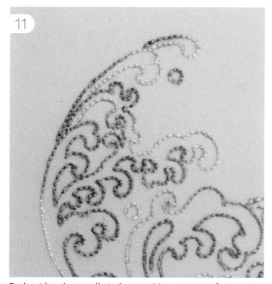

Embroider the small circle part. You can start from any position of the circle, using the starting stitch method to start, and wrap the thread on the back to end it.

The pattern is completed. Note: This pattern should not have too much white part, or it will appear fragmented. To achieve the same effect as the illustration, the selection of thread colors needs to be given particular attention. Since the backstitch is a reversed stitch, a section of a colored part requires 2–3 times the length of the thread. If the section is relatively short, the length of thread used by the starting stitch needs to be taken into consideration. If using opaque base fabric, the difficulty level is lower.

5. Satin Stitch

In traditional Chinese embroidery, there are three types of satin stitches (fig. 53): horizontal, vertical, and diagonal. The main difference lies in the direction of the needle movement. The horizontal satin stitch is worked horizontally, the vertical satin stitch is worked vertically, and the diagonal satin stitch is worked at an angle. Among them, the diagonal satin stitch allows for the most variation.

Fig. 53 Accessary of an Official Hat of Liao Dynasty (916–1125) (detail)
Unearthed from Liao dynasty tomb in Yemaotai, Faku County, Shenyang, Liaoning Province

The deer and the floral patterns on the accessary of the official hat were found to be embroidered using satin stitch technique. Known as *qizhen* in Chinese, satin stitch technique was first discovered on garments unearthed from a Western Han dynasty tomb in Mawangdui, Changsha, Hunan Province. However, due to the dominance of chain stitch embroidery, it did not see widespread use. It was not until the Wei-Jin (2nd–4th century) and Tang dynasties that the satin stitch technique started appearing frequently in embroidery, leading to the development of various other stitching methods such as encroaching satin stitch and shaded satin stitch.

Embroidery Technique

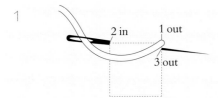

Starting stitch: The first stitch starts from one side of the pattern's edge, and the second stitch enters horizontally from the opposite side of the first stitch. Ensure that the thread is pulled tightly and aligned with the fabric surface. The third stitch is made immediately adjacent to the first stitch, exiting from the pattern's edge. Pay attention to the distance between the third and first stitches, adjusting it appropriately based on the fabric's fiber density and the thickness of the thread.

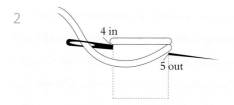

The fourth stitch is made immediately adjacent to the second stitch, entering from the pattern's edge. The fifth stitch continues next to the third stitch, exiting from the pattern's edge. Repeat this process until the entire pattern is filled.

The result is achieved with the horizontal satin stitch. The techniques for the vertical satin stitch and diagonal satin stitch are the same, with the only difference being the direction at which the stitch is made.

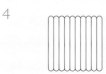

The vertical satin stitch is arranged in a vertical direction. The image above shows the result achieved with the vertical satin stitch.

The diagonal satin stitch is arranged at an angle, typically around 45–60 degrees. The angle of the stitch arrangement can be chosen and adjusted according to the pattern's requirements. The image above shows the result achieved with the diagonal satin stitch.

Tips

1. As the most important basic embroidery technique in China, satin stitch requires ensuring that the edges of the embroidered pattern are neat, smooth, and free from irregular stitch placement.
2. When working with satin stitch, it is important to master the density of thread arrangement. The threads should be neatly and smoothly arranged, avoiding sparse areas that expose the fabric and dense areas where the threads overlap and pile up.
3. Each stitch should be appropriately tightened to ensure that the thread lies flat against the fabric, but not too tight, which could cause the fabric to pucker.
4. Horizontal and vertical satin stitches should be kept parallel to their respective directions throughout the embroidery process. However, when using diagonal satin stitch, the angle of the stitch may need to be adjusted according to the twist of the pattern. Please refer to the sample project *Daisy* on page 74 for the application of diagonal satin stitch.

Embroidery Project: *Daisy*

The chrysanthemum is a renowned traditional flower in China. It has been loved and depicted by artists throughout history and praised in poetry as a symbol of the noble character of a gentleman. This artwork utilizes the daisy's flower pattern to showcase the application of the satin stitch technique, symbolizing happiness through the daisy itself.

Materials

Base fabric: white organza.
Embroidery threads: **OLYMPUS** No. 25 embroidery threads 231#, 524#, 1900#, 103# and 104# (single strand).

Steps

1 Transfer the embroidery design onto the base fabric using a heat erasable pen.

2 Use the horizontal satin stitch to embroider the central part of the flower. Start by drawing a horizontal line with the heat erasable pen at the widest part of the flower center. Use this line as a reference to draw parallel lines above and below it as auxiliary lines for the embroidery, ensuring that the stitches are not slanted or crooked.

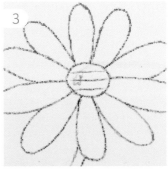

3 Using a single strand of embroidery thread 524#, start by making a starting stitch inside the flower's center.

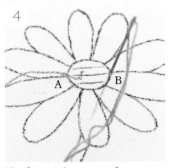

4 The first stitch goes out from one side edge (point A) of the widest part of the flower's center, and the second stitch goes in from the opposite side edge (point B).

5 Flatten the thread so that it is flush with the fabric surface. The third stitch is made next to the first stitch, coming out from the pattern's edge. The fourth stitch is made next to the second stitch, going into the fabric.

6 Use the same method to complete the upper half of the flower's center. Pay attention to keeping each thread parallel horizontally, ensuring full, accurate edges and maintaining even spacing between embroidery stitches.

7

Using the same method, complete the other half of the flower's center and make finishing stitches near the adjacent petal positions.

8

Start embroidering the petals. The petals are embroidered using three different colors of threads. Before embroidering, use a heat erasable pen to draw approximately 60-degree slanted parallel lines, using the top of the petal as the reference line. Use a single strand of embroidery thread 1900# to make starting stitches at the top of the petals.

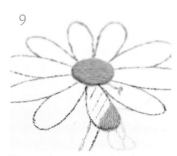

9

The petals are embroidered using diagonal satin stitches, starting from approximately one-third of the way up the petal. The direction of the stitches follows the auxiliary lines drawn earlier. Begin at one-third of the way up and fill the top of the petal with embroidery stitches, slanting toward the right (i.e. the tip of the petal).

10

After completing the top portion, return to the starting point of the first stitch and continue embroidering the remaining part of the petal. Finish off with finishing stitches on adjacent petals. Ensure that the embroidery thread remains parallel and follows the direction of the auxiliary lines throughout.

11

Embroider the petal on the right side of the petal in step 10 using thread 104#.

Embroider the remaining three petals on the right side (see the image on the right), working from bottom to top, using a single strand of thread 103#.

12

Continue embroidering the three petals on the left side using a single strand of thread 103#. Start by embroidering the middle petal with a complete shape, then proceed to embroider the upper and lower petals.

13

After completing all the petals, make finishing stitches. In this step, carefully separate the embroidery thread to expose a gap. Pass the needle through the gap for the finishing stitches, ensuring that the stitches are neatly hidden. Once the finishing stitches are done, gently smooth the embroidery thread with the needle to restore its original appearance. Be careful not to let the marks of the finishing stitches show, and do not allow the finishing thread to press down on the embroidered threads on the fabric surface.

14

Use a single strand of thread 231# to embroider the branches. When embroidering long, slender shapes, it is not necessary for each stitch to be closely adjacent to the previous one. Depending on the angle of the line, adjust the position of the stitch to ensure smooth, even shapes.

15

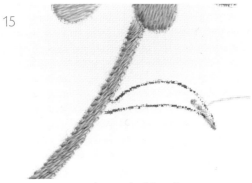

Continue using a single strand of thread 231# to embroider the leaf. After making starting stitches, start embroidering from the top of the leaf, with the entry point being along the lower contour line of the leaf. Also, pay attention to the length of the first stitch, which should cover the straighter portion near the tip of the contour line.

16

When embroidering the leaf, there is no need to draw slanted parallel lines, as the arrangement of silk grain direction in this area does not use parallel lines, but should instead vary according to the shape of the leaf. As shown in the diagram, the twisting of the thread is achieved by adjusting the distance between each stitch and the previous one. Creating smooth silk grain direction requires experimentation and practice.

17

Complete the embroidery of the leaf.

6. Knot Stitch

The knot stitch is a type of stitching technique that represents "dots" and is very important for enriching embroidery expression. It appears on unearthed artifacts from the Han dynasty, making it one of the oldest embroidery stitching techniques. Initially, the knot stitch was mainly used to depict small particles or dots. As embroidery evolved, a unique approach emerged, utilizing a large number of densely packed knot stitches to create large-scale patterns. By the Qing dynasty, the technique of extensive knot stitches had become a distinctive method in Chinese embroidery (fig. 54). Many clothing embroideries were exclusively completed using the knot technique, which is highly decorative, durable, and resistant to wear, making it widely loved.

Fig. 54 Embroidery Pattern of Butterflies and Flowers Using Knot Stitch
On this textile, there are decorative patterns of flowers and butterflies embroidered using the knot stitch technique, in blue and white colors.

Embroidery Technique

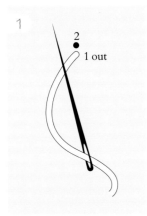

To start the stitch, knot the embroidery thread or make a starting stitch on the fabric at the desired location for knot stitch. Take the needle out from that position, pulling the entire thread through the fabric.

Hold the embroidery thread near the needle exit point with your left hand while holding the needle with your right hand. Let the embroidery thread form a loop below the needle exit point. With your left hand, wrap the embroidery thread around the needle.

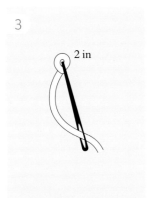

While holding the embroidery thread firmly with your left hand, vertically insert the needle into the fabric, placing the needle insertion point right next to the needle exit point, as indicated by position number 2 in reference to steps 1 and 2. Generally, it is easier to insert the needle above or to the right of the exit point. Note that when the needle is halfway through the fabric, pause and tighten the loop of thread wrapped around the needle using your left hand, ensuring that the loop sits tightly against the fabric.

Continue to insert the needle into the fabric and pull it out from the back. This completes one knot stitch.

Tips

1. If you want to create larger knots, you can use multiple strands of embroidery thread together while stitching. The more strands you use, the bigger the knot will be.

2. Another method to increase knot size is to wrap more loops of thread around the needle. For example, you can wrap 2 or 3 loops. The more loops you wrap, the larger the knot will be.

3. It is important to tightly wrap the thread loops around the needle and ensure they are snug against the fabric before pulling the needle down. If the thread loops are loose, the knots may appear fluffy and uneven in size. If the loops are not tight against the fabric, the knots will be spaced away from the fabric, resulting in unsuccessful knot stitches.

4. The choice of needle thickness in knot stitch embroidery also affects the knot size. Thicker needles create larger knots, and the hole in the center of the knot is more prominent.

Embroidery Project: *Apricot Blossom Tree*

Since the reign of Emperor Zhongzong of the Tang dynasty (656–710), after the results of the imperial examination were announced, the imperial court would organize a celebration banquet at Qujiang in Chang'an. Qujiang was adorned with apricot trees, and during their blooming season in March, the apricot blossoms created a splendid scene, giving it the name Apricot Blossom Feast. This artwork uses knot stitch embroidery to depict the vibrant scenery of apricot blossoms in full bloom during the spring season. The design is lively and attractive.

Materials

Base fabric: white organza.
Embroidery threads: **OLYMPUS** No. 25 embroidery threads 737# (single strand); 1031#, 111#, 101#, 100# and 801# (double strands).

Steps

1

Trace the embroidery design onto the base fabric using a heat erasable pen.

2

For the trunk part, roughly draw auxiliary lines using a heat erasable pen as a guide of the silk grain direction. Use 737# coffee-colored single-strand embroidery thread and stitch the main branches of the trunk using the satin stitching technique.

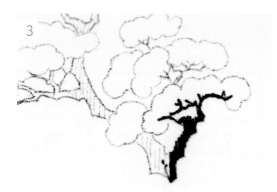

3

Use the stem stitch technique to embroider longer, thinner branches. Use short small stitches to embroider small forks. The stitching technique here can be flexibly applied.

4

Complete the embroidery of all the trunks and branches using the same method.

5

When embroidering the apricot blossoms, use a combination of 111#, 1031#, 101#, 100#, and 801# embroidery threads to create rich, varied transitions in diverse shades. First, let's demonstrate the complete stitching technique for a cluster of apricot blossoms. Use the 111# embroidery thread, take double strands and make a starting stitch near the designated green point inside the pattern's outline. Start the first stitch by exiting from the designated point and wrap the thread around the needle twice.

6

Insert the needle vertically next to the exit point, and when the needle is halfway through the fabric, tighten the thread loop and ensure it sits tightly against the fabric.

7

While keeping the thread loop unchanged (beginners can use the fingernail of their left index finger to hold the loop in place and prevent it from moving or loosening), pull the needle out from the back, gradually pulling the embroidery thread to the back to complete one knot stitch.

8

If you want to create two knot stitches that are adjacent to each other, the exit point should be approximately two thread-width gaps away from the neighboring knot stitch to avoid them being too close and causing an uneven appearance.

9

This allows the completed knot stitches to be adjacent to each other without being overly crowded.

10

As shown in the image, continue using double strands of 111# embroidery threads to create knot stitches in the lower half of this cluster of apricot blossoms. The distribution of knot stitches can be relatively free, with some clusters being denser than others. Be mindful not to arrange them too evenly and neatly.

11

Use double strands of 101# embroidery threads to create knot stitches scattered above the 111# stitches, with emphasis on specific areas if desired. As shown in the diagram, distribute more knot stitches of the 101# thread on the left side, leaving the right side for lighter colors. This way, the cluster of apricot blossoms will have a variation in shades.

12

Use double strands of 100# embroidery threads to create dispersed knot stitches in the upper part. Be sure to reserve space for white knot stitches at the top.

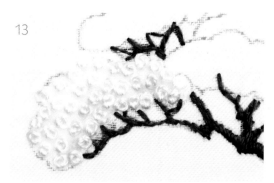

13

Use double strands of 801# embroidery threads to stitch the knot stitches at the top. The cluster of apricot flowers will exhibit a color variation with lighter shades at the top and on the right, and darker shades at the bottom and on the left, creating a spherical effect.

14

Use double strands of 801# embroidery threads for the knot stitches. When creating the knot stitches, wrap the threads around the needle only once, forming smaller stitches than the previous ones. This is done to fill the gaps at the top. The smaller knot stitches not only fill the gaps and give a fuller, more complete shape to the cluster of flowers, but also provide contrast to the larger knot stitches, making the apricot blossoms appear more abundant and lifelike.

15

Use double strands of 1031# embroidery threads to create knot stitches, embellishing the remaining gaps in the cluster of flowers. You can choose to wrap the threads around the needle once or twice for the knot stitches, depending on your preference and the specific needs of your artwork.

16

Use the same method to embroider the adjacent clusters of apricot blossoms. Pay attention to creating variations in light and dark tones within each cluster. You can also adjust the color proportions of the five embroidery threads, using more of the darker shades in some areas and more of the lighter shades in others. At the junction of the adjacent clusters, you can make the edge of the front cluster brighter and the edge of the back cluster darker to create a contrasting effect. Once you understand the distribution of light and dark tones within a cluster of apricot blossoms, you can use a heat erasable pen to draw auxiliary lines indicating the distribution on other clusters. However, during actual embroidery, you can adjust it according to the specific circumstances.

17

For convenience and reference, the following sections of the apricot blossoms will be presented by completing each color in a separate image. In the image above, we start with the knot stitches done using 111# embroidery thread.

18

Knot stitches done with 1031# embroidery thread are interspersed between the knot stitches done with 111# thread. If you prefer a lighter shade for the apricot tree, you can reduce the number of knot stitches done with 1031# thread or increase the use of single-loop knot stitches, making the darker knot stitches smaller and finer.

19

The knot stitches completed by using 101# embroidery thread are shown in the diagram above. Similarly, you can mix single-loop and double-loop knot stitches.

20

Use 100# embroidery thread to complete the knots.

21

Use 801# embroidery thread to complete the remaining knots. Along the edges of the apricot blossom cluster, you can use more single-loop knots. Check for any unsightly gaps. If there are, use an appropriate thread to make single-loop knots to fill them in. Finish the process.

7. Basic Encroaching Satin Stitch

The encroaching satin stitch technique appeared in the Tang dynasty and was an early embroidery stitch used to depict color gradation and shading (fig. 55). It was primarily used for decorative purposes in embroidery on clothing and other items. The encroaching satin stitch technique can be further divided into *fanqiangzhen* (encroaching satin stitch with hidden threads) and *zhengqiangzhen* (basic encroaching satin stitch). The basic encroaching satin stitch appeared after the chain stitch. Compared to the encroaching satin stitch with hidden threads, the boundaries where each layer of threads overlap are not as distinct, but it offers more flexibility and freedom. It is commonly used for embroidering everyday items. The basic encroaching satin stitch also served as an important foundation for the development of subsequent shaded satin stitch techniques.

Fig. 55 Double-Sided Embroidery with Peacock and Flower Tree of Tang Dynasty
The Shosoin, Nara, Japan
The technique of basic encroaching satin stitch appears on many unearthed artifacts from the Tang dynasty. Although various shaded satin stitches have been developed in later times to achieve more natural shading, basic encroaching satin stitch has always held a prominent position in Chinese embroidery for clothing and daily-use items. It continued to be widely used during the Qing dynasty, both in the practical embroidery seen in the imperial court and among the general population.

Embroidery Technique

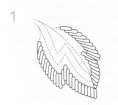

1

To start the basic encroaching satin stitch technique, move from the outer part to the inner part. Divide the design into several batches for easier completion. To facilitate understanding, auxiliary lines indicating the batches are drawn on the diagram. Use the satin stitch method to complete the first batch.

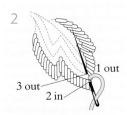

2

Starting from the second batch, use the satin stitch to cover the first batch, keeping the stitch length similar to the first batch. The first stitch of the second batch should start from the boundary auxiliary line of the second batch, and the specific stitch placement can be determined based on the pattern's shape. The second stitch should pierce into the tail end of the corresponding stitch from the first batch, with a compression of around 0.5–1 mm. The third stitch starts from beside the first stitch, and the placement point is chosen based on the shape of the pattern.

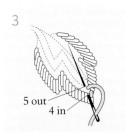

3

The fourth stitch enters beside the second stitch, piercing into the tail end of the corresponding stitch from the first batch. The fifth stitch exits beside the third stitch.

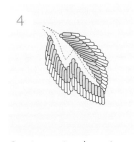

4

Continue using the satin stitch method to embroider the remaining stitches of the second batch in sequence.

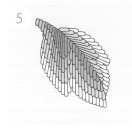

5

Use the same method to embroider the remaining stitches of the third and fourth batches. In each batch, make sure to cover on the tail end of the previous batch to ensure a neat finish without any gaps, maintaining clear layering.

Tips

1. Beginners can draw auxiliary lines to indicate the layers. However, it's important to note that in the case of basic encroaching satin stitch, strict adherence to the auxiliary lines is not necessary. The layering effect in basic encroaching satin stitching is adjusted based on the stitching technique and thread direction during the actual embroidery process. This helps to avoid a mechanical and parallel appearance.

2. Depending on the size of the pattern, the length of each stitch segment in a batch is generally around 3–6 mm. Excessively long stitches may cause the embroidery thread to loosen after removing it from the frame.

3. Basic encroaching satin stitches involve multiple layers of parallel stain stitches. Pay attention to maintaining a smooth, natural silk grain direction.

4. The fading effect of colors in basic encroaching satin stitch embroidery does not necessarily require a specific order from light to dark or vice versa. In traditional folk embroidery, vibrant, contrasting colors are often used boldly.

Embroidery Project: *Camellia*

China is the birthplace of camellia flowers. They have a graceful posture, large blossoms, and a rich, vibrant beauty. Camellias are traditional ornamental flowers in China and are also considered one of the Twelve Flower Gods. Camellias bloom in winter. During the season of tranquility and pristine white snow, their vivid red color and charming appearance are even more captivating. The enduring, evergreen nature of camellias, as well as their ability to bloom in cold weather, symbolize the endless beauty of spring. Camellias are often used in auspicious patterns due to their symbolic significance.

Materials
Base fabric: white organza.
Embroidery threads: **OLYMPUS** No. 25 embroidery threads 850#, 512#, 1021#, 140#, 141#, 142#, 261#, 253#, 254#, 255# and 736# (single strand).

Steps

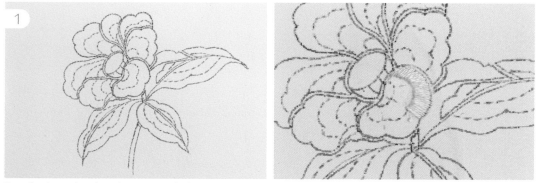

Transfer the embroidery design onto the base fabric using a heat erasable pen. Beginners can draw internal layering auxiliary lines on the pattern as a reference for embroidery. This artwork utilizes the waterway technique to create clear boundaries between the petals. When embroidering, start by stitching the complete petals first, making it easier to follow the waterway gaps while stitching the overlapping petals. Use single-strand embroidery thread 1021#. Use 2–3 small short stitches as the starting stitches on the outer layer of the middle petal and start stitching from the blank space of the first layer. Stitch outwards from the outer contour line, covering the entry point of the first layer auxiliary line, then continue with satin stitch for the first layer. You can embroider from the center toward both sides.

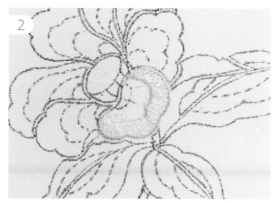

Continue stitching the other half of the first layer using satin stitch. Pay attention to the silk grain direction.

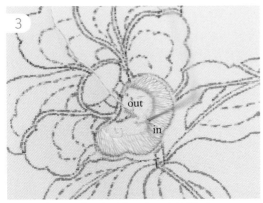

Use single-strand embroidery thread 140#. Create starting stitches on the blank space of the second layer. Stitch the second batch of threads using the satin stitch method, embroidering from the center toward both sides. As shown in the diagram, stitch outwards from the center of the second layer auxiliary line, piercing through the corresponding end of the first layer thread. Make sure to stitch along the embroidery thread to create a clear boundary.

Stitch the left side of the second layer using satin stitches. If you encounter difficulties during the turns, refer to step 3 of the *Peach* project on page 92 and use the hidden stitch technique to adjust the direction of the threads.

Stitch the right side of the second layer using the same method.

Use single-strand embroidery thread 141# to stitch the third layer.

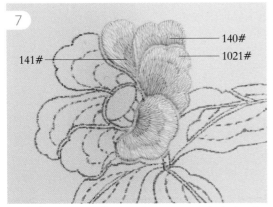

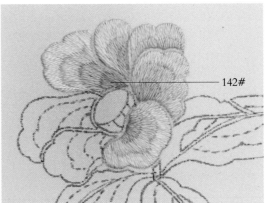

Stitch the remaining four petals in a counterclockwise direction using the same stitching method. The outer layer of each petal is stitched with 1021# thread, the second layer with 140# thread, the third layer with 141# thread, and the fourth layer of the last petal with 142# thread.

Stitch the remaining two petals in a clockwise direction, following the same color scheme as mentioned in step 7.

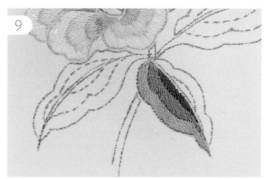

As shown in the diagram, use 253#, 254#, and 255# single-strand embroidery threads to stitch the left side of the leaves using the basic encroaching satin stitch method. The silk grain direction of the leaves is a bit more challenging to follow than that of the petals, so you can draw reference lines indicating the direction of the threads using a heat erasable pen before stitching.

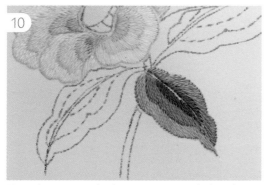

Using the same method as in step 10, stitch the other half of the leaf from the outer edge to the center using 254# and 255# single-strand embroidery threads.

Using 261# single-strand embroidery thread, stitch the tender leaf in the picture using the satin stitch method.

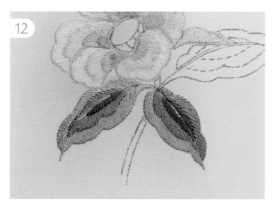

Next, using 253#, 254# and 255# single-strand embroidery threads, stitch the right half of the left leaf in three layers using the basic encroaching satin stitch method, starting from the outer edge and moving toward the inner side. Then, use 253# and 254# embroidery threads to stitch the left half of the leaf in two layers using the basic encroaching satin stitch method, also moving from the outer edge to the inner side.

Stitch the last leaf using the basic encroaching satin stitch method. Use 253#, 254# and 255# single-strand embroidery threads to stitch the lower half of the leaf from the outer edge to the inner side. Then, use 254# and 255# single-strand embroidery threads to stitch the upper half of the leaf from the outer edge to the inner side.

Using 736# single-strand embroidery thread, stitch the branches using the satin stitch method.

Stitch the white part of the flower's stamen using 850# single-strand embroidery thread. Use the satin stitch method, paying attention to the vertical direction of the threads.

Stitch the yellow part of the flower's stamen using 512# single-strand embroidery thread. Use the satin stitch method, paying attention to the horizontal direction of the threads.

Use double strands of 850# embroidery thread. Make a starting stitch at the overlap of the yellow threads. Starting from the inner edge of the yellow part of the flower's stamen, bring the double strands of threads out along the edge. Wrap the double strands of threads around the needle twice and insert it into the fabric, creating a knot. Repeat this knot stitch technique at intervals of about 1.5 mm, forming a circle around the yellow part of the stamen. Fill the empty space in the center with two knots, ensuring even spacing. Finish off with a finishing stitch.

8. Encroaching Satin Stitch with Hidden Threads

The encroaching satin stitch with hidden threads creates a clearer, more distinct layered effect, making it more decorative and unique in Chinese folk embroidery (fig. 56). It involves a special technique called Y-shaped loop stitching (see the Embroidery Technique on next page). It is commonly used to depict flower petals, butterflies, and other traditional decorative patterns. When representing irregular curves like waves, a stem stitch is used instead of the Y-shaped loop stitching. This technique is also used in European embroidery, where it is typically used for outlining patterns to emphasize the pattern's edges, rather than for creating layered shading within the pattern.

Fig. 56 Embroidered Panel of Ming Dynasty
The Metropolitan Museum of Art, New York
In the depicted embroidery, you can see the full, clear layers of peony petals in the center. Each layer has a slightly raised texture, which is characteristic of the encroaching satin stitch with hidden threads technique.

Embroidery Technique

1

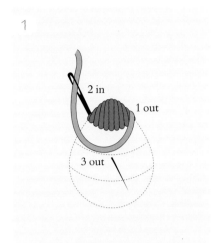

To start the encroaching satin stitch with hidden threads, the pattern should be divided into several evenly spaced layers. Use auxiliary lines as a guide. Begin by stitching the first layer, coming up along the outer contour line and going down to cover the first auxiliary line. Then, as shown in the illustration, create the characteristic Y shape of the encroaching satin stitch with hidden threads. The first stitch comes up from the outer edge of one side of the thread bundle, slightly above the auxiliary line. The second stitch goes down from the other side, at the same height as the first stitch. The third stitch comes up below the center point of the second auxiliary line.

2

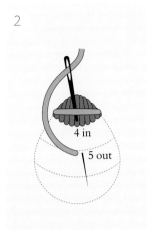

The fourth stitch crosses over the horizontal line, piercing through the tail of the center thread of the first layer, and then tightening the thread to bring the lowest point of the horizontal line to the position of the auxiliary line. The fifth stitch is placed closely next to the third stitch and comes up from below the auxiliary line.

3

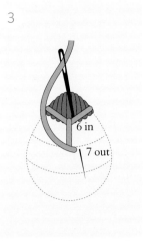

As seen in the illustration, after the fourth stitch is inserted and the thread is tightened, the original horizontal line forms a V shape. The sixth stitch is placed closely next to the fourth stitch, and when inserting the needle, it should be slanted toward the inside of the stitch to pull the thread to the position of the auxiliary line. The seventh stitch is placed closely next to the fifth stitch and comes up from below the auxiliary line.

4

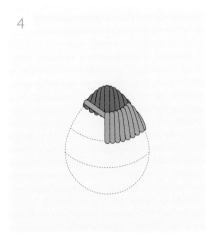

Following the above steps, continue embroidering the right side of the second layer from the center to the outer edge. After completing it, a clear boundary is formed where the right side intersects with the first layer, and the arc appears smooth.

5

Continue from the left side of the center line of the second layer and repeat the above steps to embroider the left side, completing the second layer.

6

After completing the second layer, there is a smooth, complete arc boundary between the first and second layer, and you can clearly see that the edge of the arc slightly bulges, creating a noticeable decorative effect.

7

Use the same method to complete the embroidery of the third and fourth layer. Before embroidering each layer, make sure to secure the thread. Also, pay attention to the direction of the grain for each layer while embroidering.

Tips

1. Ensure the outer contour of the pattern is neat and pay attention to arranging the stitching direction based on the pattern's characteristics.
2. The distance between the auxiliary line and the high points of the Y-shaped looping stitches on the left and right, depends on the size of the entire design. The larger the design, the farther the needle points will be from the auxiliary line.
3. For the encroaching satin stitch with hidden threads, starting from the second layer, the arc boundary formed by each layer is not determined by the needle insertion points but by the pulling force of the embroidery thread angled inward toward the horizontal lines (as shown in step 3 on page 90). This helps adjust the horizontal lines to create the desired curvature of the pattern.
4. The auxiliary line is covered by the previous layer of stitches, so it's important to maintain a consistent shape when covering the auxiliary line with stitches. This ensures a clear shape for reference when stitching the next layer, forming the edge of the arc.
5. If you encounter a wavy boundary line, use the stem stitch instead of the Y-shaped looping stitches. This means creating a wavy line at the boundary using the stem stitch, and then stitching the next layer tightly against the wavy line. This will also create a clear and slightly raised layered effect along the edge.

Embroidery Project: *Peach*

In Chinese mythology, peaches are considered the fruit of the immortals, believed to bestow longevity upon those who consume them. Therefore, they are associated with the auspicious concept of longevity. The unique shape of peaches lends itself well to the encroaching satin stitch with hidden threads technique, making it an ideal subject for this small demonstration piece.

Materials
Base fabric: white organza.
Embroidery threads: **OLYMPUS** No. 25 embroidery threads 155#, 105#, 104#, 103#, 102#, 101#, 100#, 221#, 220#, 2502#, 2251 and 745# (single strand).

Steps

Trace the embroidery design onto the fabric using a heat erasable pen. The horizontal curved lines within the peach represent the boundaries between different shades, dividing the peach into 7 layers. The vertical lines serve as auxiliary lines for the direction of the embroidery stitches in each layer.

Using 155# single-strand embroidery thread, start stitching at the tip of the peach where the first layer is blank, using 2–3 small short stitches. The first stitch should come out from below the central point of the first layer's curved boundary, encompassing the auxiliary line within the stitch. The second stitch should enter from the central point of the outer contour, and the entry point can be slightly outside the contour line. This will result in a fuller shape for the peach's tip.

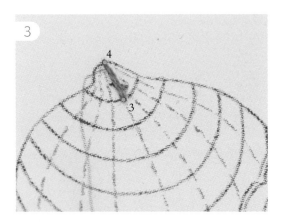

Since the tip of the peach has a distinct shape with a narrow upper part and a wider lower part, there are some considerations when stitching with satin stitch. First, when coming out from the side of the layer's auxiliary line, the exit points can be slightly spread apart, but avoid leaving any gaps. When entering along the contour line of the peach's tip, each entry point can be closer together. Additionally, you can make a "hidden stitch" between two regular stitches to fill the gap between the narrow and wide parts. In the diagram, after the third stitch comes out to the right of the first stitch, the fourth stitch enters approximately 1 mm away from the outer contour, creating a hidden stitch.

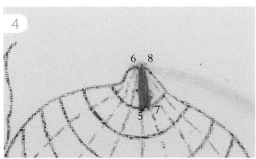

In the diagram, the fifth stitch comes out next to the third stitch, and the sixth stitch enters right next to the second stitch. The seventh stitch comes out next to the fifth stitch, and the eighth stitch enters approximately 1 mm away from the outer contour, creating another hidden stitch.

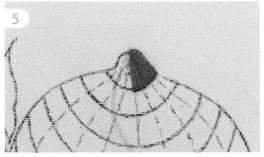

Adjust the direction of the stitches according to the actual needs and individual stitching habits by using hidden stitches. Complete the stitching of the right side of the first layer. Pay attention to keeping the outer contour neat and smooth and ensure that the curved auxiliary line are covered by the stitches, with the lower edge of the stitches following the shape of the auxiliary line.

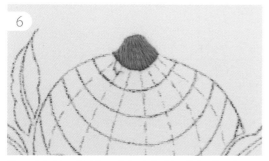

Complete the stitching of the left side of the first layer using the same method.

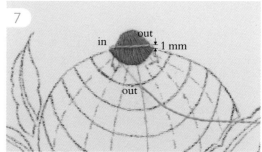

Use 105# thread to make 3 small stitches at the beginning of the second layer. Start by stitching out from the right outer edge of the first batch of stitches, with the stitch point about 1 mm higher than the edge of the stitches. Enter the corresponding position from the left side and pull the thread to create a horizontal line. Then stitch out from below the center point of the curved auxiliary line of the second layer. Please note that references to the center point in the following instructions indicate the intersection point between the central vertical auxiliary line (as shown in green) and the curved boundary line of the peach pattern.

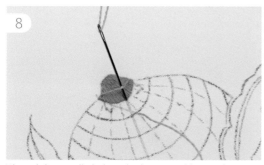

Thread the needle below the horizontal line and enter from the bottom center point of the first batch of stitches. Please note that the entry point can be stitched at the end of the previous batch of stitches or right next to it.

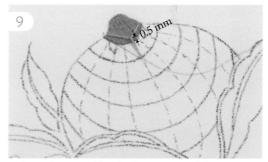

Tighten the vertical line at the center until the horizontal line is pulled into a V shape, with the lowest point near the bottom edge of the first batch of stitches, at a distance of approximately 0.5 mm.

Continue stitching from the center line toward the right side. Each exit stitch should be made below the arc dividing line, and when entering, cross over the horizontal line and insert the needle downward and inward. Maintain consistency with the previous stitch in terms of the stitch placement. After each stitch is made, tighten the thread to ensure that the horizontal line aligns with the curvature of the arc dividing line.

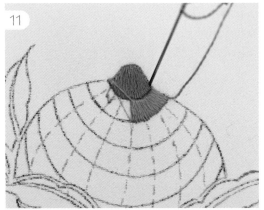

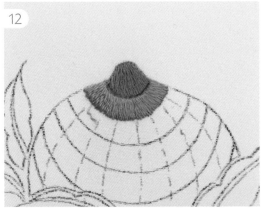

Complete the stitching for the right side of the second batch. The last stitch can be made inside the horizontal line or placed closely outside the horizontal line of the first batch, taking care to maintain the overall aesthetic of the design.

Use the same method to complete the stitching for the left side of the second batch. At this point, the boundary line between the first and second batches should form a smooth, rounded curve, appearing full and seamless without visible needle points.

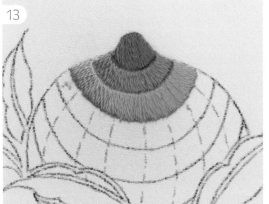

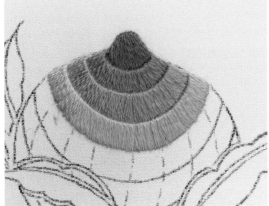

For the third and fourth batches, continue using the same method with 104# and 103# single-strand embroidery threads to complete the stitching. Follow the steps described earlier to achieve the desired results.

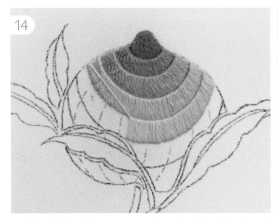

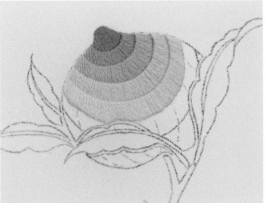

For the fifth batch, use 102# embroidery thread. Follow the same method of creating the horizontal lines and stitching techniques as before. However, there is a design element in this pattern that incorporates a traditional Chinese embroidery technique called waterway. This means that there is a gap or space between the peach and the leaf, and this is represented by two parallel lines in the pattern to indicate the outline of each shape. When stitching, treat these lines as the outer contour lines and stitch accordingly.

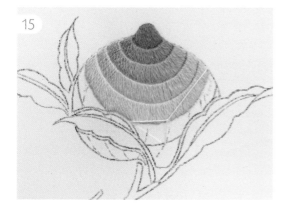

Use 101# embroidery thread to finish the sixth batch. For this batch, which is divided into two parts by the leaf, use the same technique of Y-shaped looped stitches. The position of the horizontal line and the points on the right side is shown in the diagram. In this case, there is no center position for the looped stitches because the distance to the leaf is too short, making it difficult to manage. Instead, the indicated position provides a wider space, which allows for better tension. Therefore, the position of the looped stitches can be adjusted based on the actual situation and doesn't have to be strictly centered.

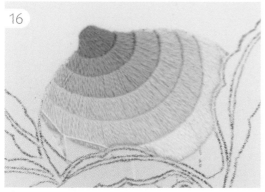

The position of the horizontal line and the points on the left side of the sixth batch is shown in the diagram.

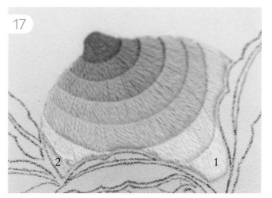

After completing the sixth batch, use 100# embroidery thread to stitch the seventh batch. The seventh batch is divided into four parts (1, 2, 3, 4) as shown in the steps 17 to 19. You can start by stitching the larger right portion 1 and then move to the smaller left portion. The Y-shaped looped stitching technique for the left portion 2 is shown in the diagram. When stitching the pointed corners, extra care should be taken. In this case, the horizontal line is short, so it is important to tighten it to avoid loose loops. Pay attention to the tension applied in each stitch to maintain a perfect curve.

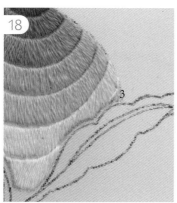

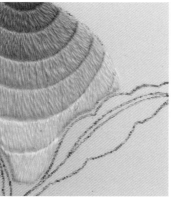

For the small pointed corner on the far right (see portion 3), the Y-shaped looped stitching technique is applied as shown in the diagram. The instructions are the same as in step 17. However, due to the extremely small area, it is also acceptable to skip the looped stitching in this section, if the technique is beyond your abilities.

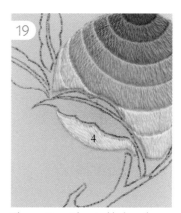

The portion 4 located below the leaf in the seventh batch does not require Y-shaped looped stitching. You can simply use satin stitch to complete it.

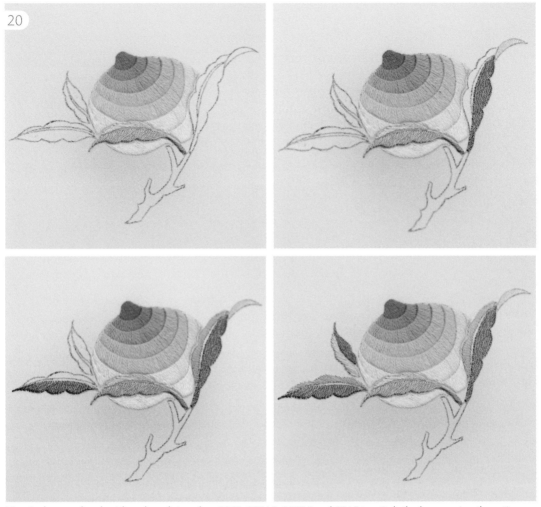

Use single-strand embroidery threads in colors 220#, 2251#, 2502# and 221# to stitch the leaves using the satin stitch technique. When stitching the leaves, adjust the direction of the stitches using the hidden stitch technique described in step 3 to ensure a smooth flow of the silk grain direction.

Finally, use a single strand of embroidery thread in color 745# to stitch the branches. Divide the branches into the main stem and three small branches, and use the satin stitch technique to embroider them. Refer to the diagram for the direction of the stitches.

9. Regular Shaded Satin Stitch

The history of the regular shaded satin stitch is very ancient and can be traced back to the artifacts unearthed from the Han dynasty Mawangdui (fig. 57). It is also the basic stitching technique used in Chinese double-sided embroidery. The relative simple regular shaded satin stitch involves filling the fabric layer by layer with threads, allowing for monochromatic or multicolored designs. When depicting color blending, the regular shaded satin stitch creates a more natural, delicate effect compared to the encroaching satin stitch. The regular shaded satin stitch was widely used and remained a common embroidery technique for clothing and accessories until the end of the Qing dynasty. Subsequent techniques such as the double shaded satin stitch, the round shaded satin stitch, and the long and short shaded satin stitch all evolved from the regular shaded satin stitch.

Fig. 57 *Han Dynasty Embroidery*
Excavated from Tomb No. 1 in Mawangdui, Changsha, Hunan Province
The embroidery patterns in the picture were all created using the regular shaded satin stitch technique.

Embroidery Technique

1

As shown in the picture, the first batch is embroidered along the outline. The stitches should be one long and one short, and the shorter stitches are approximately half a length longer than the longer stitches. Generally, embroidery starts from the middle of the pattern making it easier to control the direction and length of the stitches.

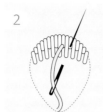

2

The second batch continues from the middle position, with each stitch being inserted between the two longer stitches of the first batch, passing through the tail end of the short stitches of the first batch. The length of the stitches in the second batch is similar to that of the longer stitches in the first batch.

3

The completed state of the second batch is shown in the picture.

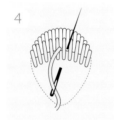

4

In the third batch, all the stitches are inserted into the gaps between the stitches of the second batch, passing through the tail ends of the longer stitches from the first batch. The length of the stitches in the third batch is similar to the previous ones.

5

The completed state of the third batch is shown in the picture.

6

According to the pattern, continue embroidering batch by batch using the method described above until the entire pattern is filled.

Tips

1. Following the traditional Chinese regular shaded satin stitch technique, the first batch of threads does not differentiate between long and short stitches. Instead, each thread is slightly separated to facilitate the insertion of the second batch of threads. However, since this book demonstrates the use of cotton thread instead of the finer silk thread traditionally used in Chinese embroidery, the larger gap required for cotton thread results in the first batch of threads appearing sparse. Therefore, it is necessary to add short stitches between the long stitches to ensure a dense appearance in the first batch of threads.

2. When arranging the threads, always pay attention to the silk grain direction, allowing each batch of threads to transition smoothly.

3. During transitions or changes in the shape of the pattern, adjust the length of the stitches flexibly. However, in general, the length of the stitches in the regular shaded satin stitch technique does not vary significantly except for the last batch.

4. When embroidering with the regular shaded satin stitch technique, you can use a single color or multiple colors. Each batch can have a different color, or you can change colors every two or more batches, depending on the color variations required by the pattern.

Embroidery Project: *Plum Blossoms*

The plum blossom, along with orchids, bamboo, and chrysanthemums, are collectively known as the Four Gentlemen. It is also called the Three Friends of Winter, along with pine and bamboo. The plum blossom, with its noble, resilient, and humble character, inspires people to strive and work hard. In the harsh winter, plum blossoms bloom before all other flowers, symbolizing the arrival of spring. This artwork uses the regular shaded satin stitch technique to depict blooming plum blossoms.

Materials
Base fabric: white organza.
Embroidery threads: **OLYMPUS** No. 25 embroidery threads 501# (double strands); 520#, 101#, 102#, 103#, 123#, 124#, 125#, 126#, 154#, 155#, 156#, 1085#, 212#, 216#, 714# and 1029# (single strand).

Steps

Trace the embroidery design and auxiliary lines onto the fabric using a heat erasable pen. The circular arcs serve as reference lines for layering the threads, while the auxiliary lines converging toward the flower core indicate the center lines of the petals.

Embroider with a single strand of 101# thread, starting from the outer edge of the petal. After marking the starting point, bring the needle out from the outline and follow the direction of the auxiliary line, indicating the center of the petal. Insert the needle along the second layering arc line and embroider a long stitch.

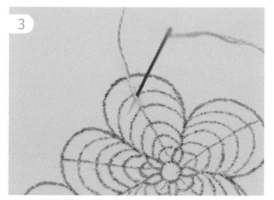

Next to the first long stitch, bring the needle out from the outline and insert it along the first arc line, embroidering a short stitch.

Embroider by alternating between long and short stitches, completing the right half of the petal.

Embroider the left half of the petal using the same method.

Embroider the remaining four petals one by one.

Embroider the second batch using a single strand of 103# thread. After marking the starting stitch in the blank area, insert the needle between the two long stitches of the first batch, coming out from the tail of the short stitch.

Each stitch in the second batch comes out between the long stitches of the first batch, from the tail of the short stitches. Insert the needle along the third layering arc line. After embroidering half of the petal from the center toward one side, return to the center and embroider the other half toward the opposite side.

Embroider the second batch of the remaining four petals using the same method.

Embroider the third batch using a single strand of 123# thread, coming out between the two stitches of the second batch, from the tail of the long stitches of the first batch. Insert the needle along the fourth arc line. Like the previous batches, embroider one side of the petal and then the other side to complete the entire petal.

Embroider the third batch of the remaining four petals using the same method.

Embroider the fourth batch using a single strand of 124# thread, coming out between the two stitches of the third batch, from the tail of the thread from the second batch. Insert the needle along the fifth arc line. Like the previous batches, embroider all five petals using the same method.

Embroider the fifth batch using a single strand of 125# thread. Since the fourth batch of stitches is already dense, it may be difficult to see the tail positions of the third batch. In this case, you can bring the needle out from between the two stitches of the fourth batch, approximately at the midpoint of the fourth batch's thread, and insert the needle while pressing along the circular contour line in the center.

When embroidering this batch, ensure that the needle point covers the outline of the central circle.

As shown in the picture, complete the embroidery of the fifth batch.

Using a single strand of 126# thread, bring the needle out from approximately halfway through the fifth batch. Embroider a few stitches in each petal, deepening the center of the petal to create richer color gradients.

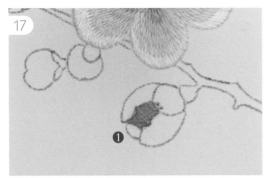

Embroider the satin stitch using a single strand of 155# thread to fill in the central part of the large bud (No. 1). Press the stitches along the outline while embroidering.

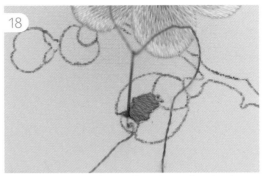

Use a single strand of 154# thread to embroider the smallest petal at the bottom. Make a starting stitch in the blank area and bring the needle out from the outer contour line. When inserting the needle, cover a bit of the edge of the embroidered center part. This technique ensures that there are no gaps between two adjacent shapes.

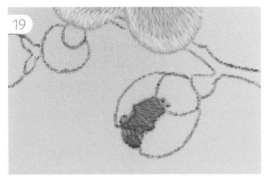

Embroider the first batch of the small petal using the regular shaded satin stitch technique.

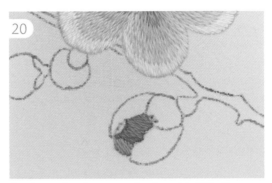

Continue using the same color thread to fill in the remaining gaps. Although the area is small, using the regular shaded satin stitch technique can create smoother curves and better depict the petal's transitions compared to the satin stitch.

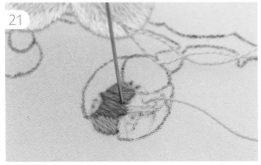

Use single-strand thread 102# to stitch the first batch of adjacent petals. Before stitching, as shown in the diagram, draw three layers of auxiliary lines with a central auxiliary line on the petals. Start stitching from the middle of the petal, using long and short stitches for the first batch. When the stitch needs to overlap with the adjacent stitched area, you can stitch by coming out from the inside and going in from the adjacent pattern's line. This method helps ensure more accuracy and ease in following the contour lines.

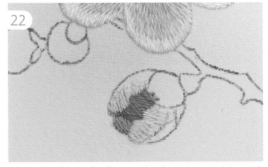

After completing the first batch of stitches on this petal using the regular shaded satin stitch technique, you can proceed to stitch the first batch of the opposite petal as well.

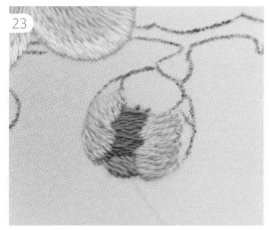

Using the 124# embroidery thread, proceed to stitch the second batch following the same method as the previous floral embroidery techniques.

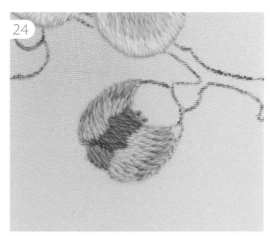

Use the 125# single-strand embroidery thread to stitch the third batch for the two petals.

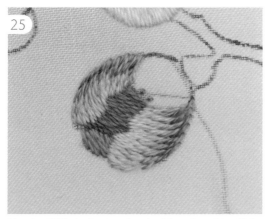

Use the 126# single-strand embroidery thread to stitch the fourth batch for the two petals.

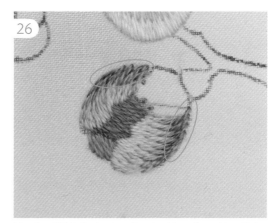

Use the 155# single-strand embroidery thread to stitch the last section (green circle area) following the silk grain direction. This will enhance the color saturation and complement the color of the center petals.

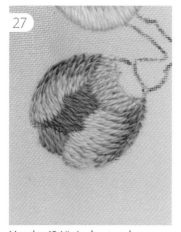

Use the 124# single-strand embroidery thread to stitch the first batch of the remaining petal.

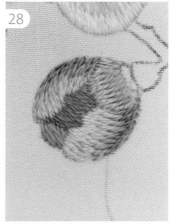

Use the 125# single-strand embroidery thread to stitch the second batch.

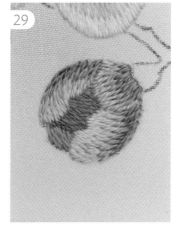

Use the 126# single-strand embroidery thread to stitch the third batch.

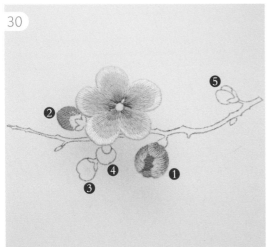

Use the 154# single-strand embroidery thread to stitch the first batch of No. 2 bud.

Use the 155# single-strand embroidery thread to stitch the second batch of the No. 2 bud and the first batch of No. 3 bud.

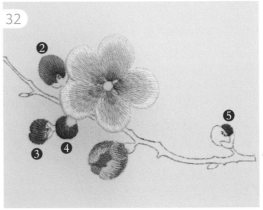

Use the 156# single-strand embroidery thread to stitch the third batch of No. 2 bud, the second batch of No. 3 bud, and the first batch of No. 4 bud. The right petal of No. 5 bud will be stitched using the satin stitch.

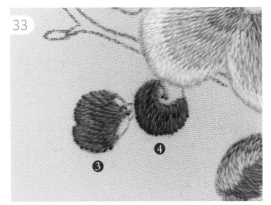

Continue using the 156# single-strand embroidery thread to stitch the third batch of No. 3 bud, filling it completely. Use the 1085# single-strand embroidery thread to stitch the second batch of No. 4 bud, filling it completely.

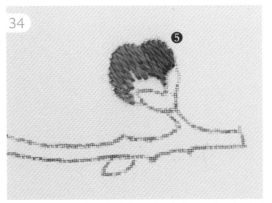

Use the 155# embroidery thread and the regular shaded satin stitch to embroider the first batch of the left petal of No. 5 bud.

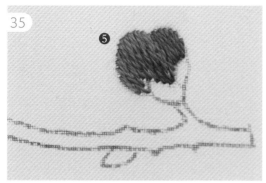

Use the 156# single-strand embroidery thread to embroider the second batch of No. 5 bud.

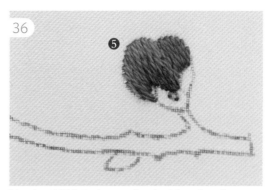

Use the 1085# single-strand embroidery thread to embroider the third batch and fill the petal completely of No. 5 bud.

Use the 714# single-strand embroidery thread and employ the satin stitch technique to embroider the branch part.

Use the 1029# single-strand embroidery thread and employ the satin stitch technique to embroider the sepals of the bud.

Use the 216# single-strand embroidery thread to embroider the dark green leaf buds on the branches using the satin stitch technique. Then, switch to the 212# single-strand thread to embroider the central part of the plum blossom. Start by using the satin stitch to embroider five small green petals, and then embroider the central circular part. Be careful to overlap the edges of the previously embroidered sections, ensuring there are no gaps between them.

Use the 501# double-strand embroidery threads to create single-loop knot stitches as the yellow part of the flower stamen. Then, switch to the 520# single-strand thread and follow the illustration to connect the yellow knot stitches with the central green part. The entire design is completed.

10. Round Shaded Satin Stitch

Round shaded satin stitch is a variation of the regular shaded satin stitch technique used in embroidery, primarily for stitching circular or elliptical patterns. In the round shaded satin stitch technique, all the thread lines converge toward the center of the circle, with the outermost circle having the highest number of stitches. Subsequent batches have decreasing numbers of stitches, and as the stitching progresses towards the center, the thread lines converge at the center point. The round shaded satin stitch technique is commonly used to depict large circular shapes and is often seen in extant dragon robes from the Ming and Qing dynasties (fig. 58).

Fig. 58 Colored Embroidery Dragon Canopy of Qing Dynasty (detail)

The dragon ball patterns on the dragon robe are typically embroidered with the round shaded satin stitch technique, in addition to the use of goldwork embroidery. Since it is challenging to handle the convergence at the center of the design when using the round shaded satin stitch, a flame pattern is often used to cover the central part of the dragon ball, avoiding the convergence point at the center.

The image on the right shows a curtain embroidered with a dragon. The body of the dragon is embroidered with golden thread, while the dragon ball is created using the round shaded satin stitch technique.

Embroidery Technique

1

As shown in the diagram, draw four layers of auxiliary lines evenly spaced within the circle. The actual number of auxiliary lines may vary during the embroidery process, depending on the design.

2

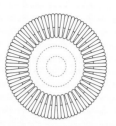

Stitch along the circular outline, using alternating long and short stitches to create the first batch. For the short stitches, insert the needle while pressing against the first auxiliary line, and for the long stitches, insert the needle while pressing against the second auxiliary line. All stitches should converge toward the center of the circle.

3

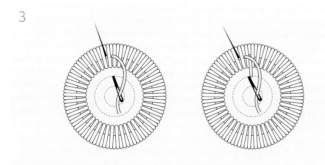

Begin all the stitches of the second batch between the long stitches of the first batch. Bring the needle out at the tail end of the short stitches of the first batch, while covering them slightly. Insert the needle while pressing against the third auxiliary line.

4

After completing the second batch, begin all the stitches of the third batch in the gaps between the stitches of the second batch. Bring the needle out from the tail end of the long stitches of the first batch, while inserting the needle as you press against the central (fourth) auxiliary line.

5

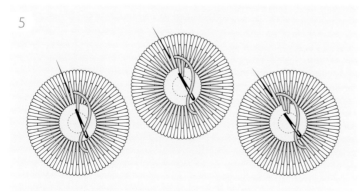

Starting from the third layer, you can use the hidden stitch technique to reduce the density of stitches pressed against the fourth auxiliary line. The hidden stitch can be done by hiding one or two stitches.

6

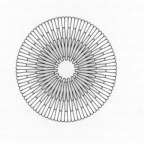

Complete the embroidery of the third layer of stitches.

7

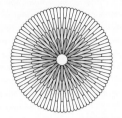

When inserting the fourth layer of stitches between the third layer, it can be challenging to find the end of the second layer of stitches due to the density of the third layer. In such cases, you can generally start the fourth layer of stitches approximately halfway between the third layer's stitches. When inserting the needle, aim to stitch close to the center, but not directly on it. The fourth layer of stitches can be adjusted based on the specific situation, including reducing the number of stitches or using the hidden stitch technique. The illustration demonstrates the technique of reducing stitches, skipping one gap between the third layer's stitches instead of inserting a stitch in every gap. This technique is known as reducing stitches.

8

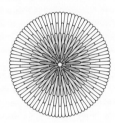

Insert short stitches between the fourth layer of stitches. When inserting them, stitch toward the center.

9

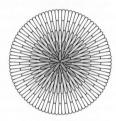

According to the pattern, make a few short stitches to fill the holes made by stitching into the center.

Tips

1. Following the traditional Chinese method of round shaded satin stitch, the first batch of stitches does not distinguish between long and short stitches. Instead, each thread is spaced slightly apart to facilitate the insertion of the second batch of stitches. However, since we are using cotton thread instead of fine silk thread traditionally used in Chinese embroidery, the required spacing for cotton thread will be larger, resulting in the first batch of stitches appearing too sparse. It is thus necessary to add short stitches between long stitches to ensure a dense feel for the first batch of stitches.

2. Starting from the third batch, you can adjust the number of stitches and hide stitches according to the pattern. The process of reducing stitches and hiding stitches does not necessarily need to strictly follow the above steps, but can be handled flexibly.

3. When hiding two stitches, depending on the situation, if a tighter concealment is needed, the second hidden stitch can be slightly shorter than the first one, closer to the first hidden stitch. This allows for a more concealed hiding and reduces the required space.

4. The circles formed by the stitches in each batch should be kept relatively round.

Embroidery Project: *Dragon Ball*

The court robe was the most magnificent ceremonial attire of the emperor in the Qing dynasty. On important ceremonies and rituals, the emperor wore the court robe. During the Ming and Qing dynasties, Chinese weaving techniques reached their peak, and royal garments were the culmination of top craftsmanship, incorporating twelve different patterns. Among them, the flame pattern represented energy and illumination. The flames curl upwards from the bottom, symbolizing the people's hearts turning toward the monarch. This artwork showcases the flame pattern as a backdrop for the Dragon Ball, demonstrating the ingenious use of the round shaded satin stitch technique in traditional Chinese attire.

Materials

Base fabric: white organza.
Embroidery threads: **OLYMPUS** No. 25 embroidery threads 850#, 520#, 5205#, 1052#, 1051# and 535# (single strand).

Steps

Draw the embroidery design and auxiliary lines on the base fabric using a heat erasable pen. The circular auxiliary lines are reference lines for thread layering and the lines converging toward the center of the circle indicate the silk grain direction.

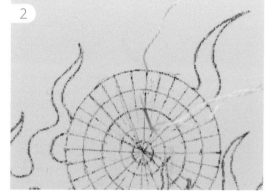

Start embroidering from the outermost circle using 850# single-strand embroidery thread. Once you have made the starting stitch, bring the needle out from the outer contour line, following the direction indicated by the auxiliary lines. Press the needle against the second circular auxiliary line and make a long stitch.

Place the second stitch right next to the first long stitch. Bring the needle out from the contour line, pressing against the first auxiliary line, and make a short stitch.

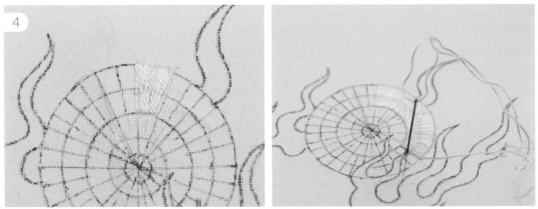

Continue embroidering with alternating long and short stitches until you reach the flame pattern. In the illustration, the pointed edge of the flame pattern falls between the first and second auxiliary lines. You can continue making short stitches as usual, while the long stitches should be inserted along the edges of the flame pattern.

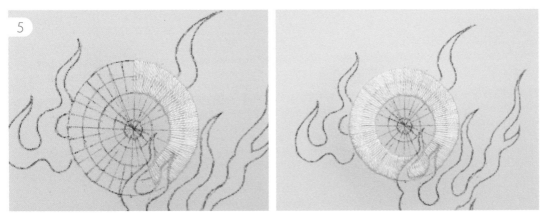

Skip over the flame pattern and continue in the same direction as the long stitches in the upper half. From the opposite edge of the flame pattern, come out with the needle and insert it along the second auxiliary line to continue embroidering the interrupted long stitch. Next, using the same method, whether it's a long or short stitch, continue to skip over the flame pattern while maintaining the convergence toward the center point.

Complete the first batch of embroidery.

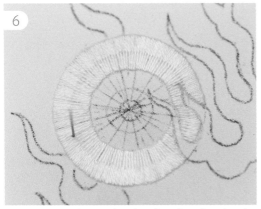

Using 520# single-strand embroidery thread, embroider the second batch. After making the starting stitch in the blank area, insert the needle between the two long stitches of the first batch, coming out from the tail of the short stitch.

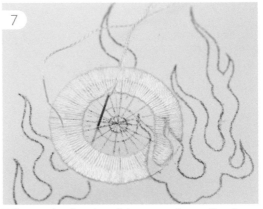

Following the direction of the converging auxiliary lines, press down on the third circular auxiliary line and insert the needle.

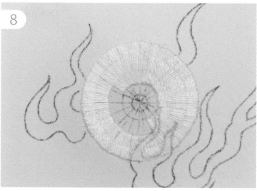

Following the same method as described above, insert one stitch between each pair of long threads and continue embroidering the second batch until encountering the flame pattern. As in the first batch, when blocked by the flame, skip the obstructed portion and maintain the thread direction converging toward the center while embroidering the second batch.

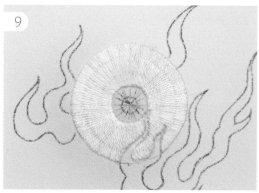

Complete the second batch of embroidery.

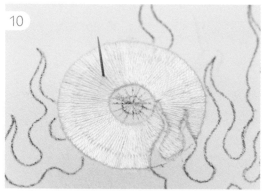

Using single-strand embroidery thread in color 5205#, embroider the third batch. Make a starting stitch in the blank area and start the stitch from the tail end of the long stitches in the first batch.

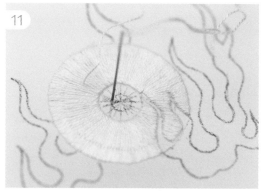

Begin the stitch by pressing against the fourth circular auxiliary line.

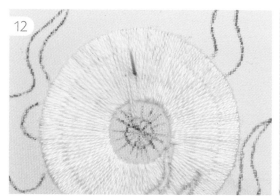

Due to the intensified convergence effect starting from the third layer, there is a significant difference in circumference between the third and fourth circular auxiliary lines. When embroidering the third batch, it is possible to reduce the number of stitches as needed. As shown in the diagram, instead of inserting a stitch in each gap between two threads of the second batch, a stitch is skipped here, and the third stitch of the third batch is directly embroidered from the fourth gap. This reduces the number of stitches by one.

The effect of reducing stitches between the second and third stitches is shown in the diagram on the right.

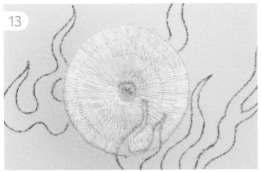

13

Make appropriate reductions in stitches as needed based on the pattern to complete the embroidery of the third batch. When encountering the flame pattern, handle it in the same way as before.

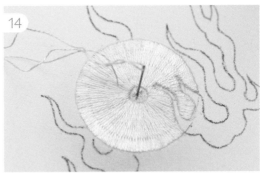

14

Continue using the single strand of 5205# embroidery thread to embroider the fourth batch. At this point, it is difficult to see the tail end of the second batch of threads. The stitch comes out slightly above the midpoint of the third batch of threads, still between the gaps of the two threads. The entry point of the stitch is close to the center, maintaining the consistent thread direction as in the previous batches.

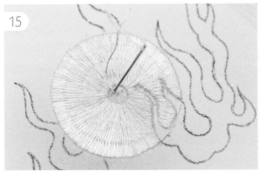

15

While reducing stitches in the fourth batch, it is also possible to incorporate hidden stitches. As shown in the diagram, one stitch is skipped between the first and second stitches, representing a stitch reduction. At the same time, the entry point of the second stitch is adjacent to the first stitch, but slightly shorter, indicating a hidden stitch. This helps to reduce the number of stitches accumulating at the center, preventing excessive thickness at the center point.

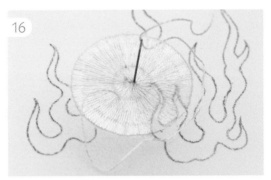

16

When halfway through the fourth batch, a hole may form at the center due to multiple stitches converging. When stitching the remaining half of the circle, the entry points of some stitches can be placed across the hole, inserted through the opposite end of the stitching thread. This way, stitch by stitch, the hole can be covered up.

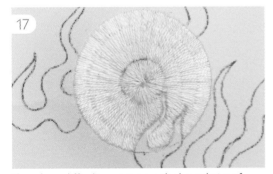

17

If you have difficulty maintaining the boundaries of the circle while stitching the fourth batch, you can use a heat erasable pen to draw auxiliary lines. The image shows the result after completing the fourth batch of stitching.

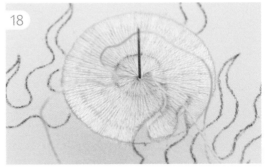

18

After completing the fourth batch of stitching, the center may appear uneven in thickness. To further conceal the convergence point in the center and make the fourth batch look more complete, you can add a few short stitches that converge toward the center.

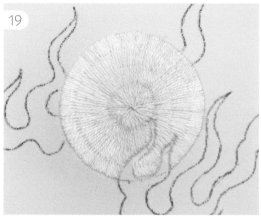

The result after embellishing with short stitches can be viewed alongside step 18 for comparison.

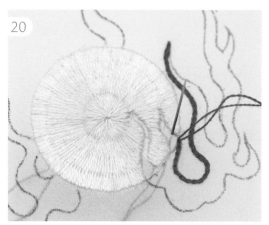

Using single-strand embroidery thread in color 1052#, use the chain stitch method to embroider the outermost part of the flame. When encountering the previously embroidered interior of the circular shape, continue embroidering along the contour lines of the flame.

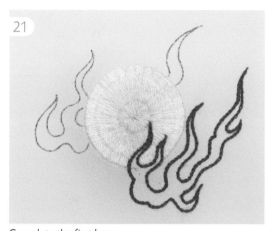

Complete the first layer.

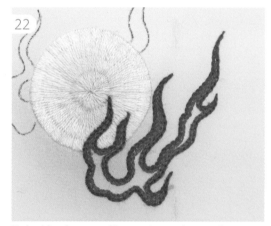

Embroider the second layer using single-strand embroidery thread in color 1051#.

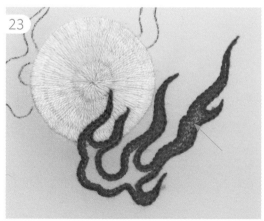

Embroider the section indicated by the arrow in the diagram using single-strand embroidery thread 535#.

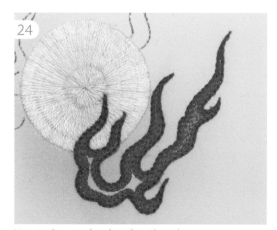

Use single-strand embroidery thread 1051# to embroider another round as shown in the picture.

25

Fill the remaining gaps with embroidery thread 535#.

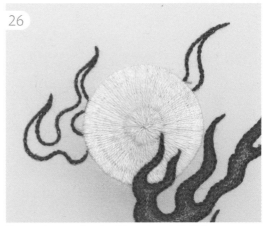

26

Use single-strand embroidery thread 1052# to embroider the outer edges of two additional clusters of flames.

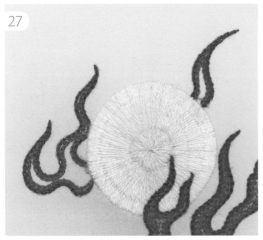

27

Use single-strand embroidery thread 1051# to embroider the second round of two clusters of flames.

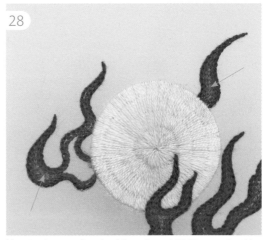

28

Use single-strand embroidery thread 535# to embroider the gaps indicated by the arrows in the picture.

29

Use single-strand embroidery thread 1051# to embroider another round at the location indicated by the arrow in the picture.

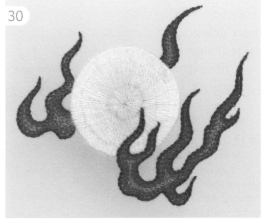

30

Use single-strand embroidery thread 535# to fill in the remaining blank space and complete all the embroidery.

11. Long and Short Shaded Satin Stitch

The long and short shaded satin stitch is the most commonly used and widely applied stitch in Chinese decorative embroidery (fig. 59). The arrangement of lines in the long and short shaded satin stitch is irregular, with needles interlocking and layers overlapping. When embroidering, the arrangement of lines can be flexible and varied. As a result, the long and short shaded satin stitch can effectively depict the silk texture and transitions of the embroidery subject. It is more delicate and natural in representing color changes than the regular shaded satin stitch, leaving no trace and creating a strong artistic expression.

Fig. 59 *Washing the Horse*
Palace Museum, Beijing
This is a representative embroidery artwork by the Ming dynasty embroiderer Han Ximeng. It was created by imitating the brushwork of painting on white silk satin using needle embroidery. The white horse in the picture is depicted using the long and short shaded satin stitch to present the texture of its muscles, resulting in a vivid, lifelike portrayal.

The long and short shaded satin stitch was a later development of stitch techniques, and its exact origin is difficult to determine. However, the introduction of the long and short shaded satin stitch elevated the level of color transitions in embroidery, making it commonly used in depicting flowers, plants, animals, figures, and other things in decorative embroidery. To fully showcase the advantages and charm of the long and short shaded satin stitch, it is necessary to use finely split Chinese silk embroidery thread, achieving seamless layering and smooth color transitions without showing needle marks. This book explains and demonstrates the use of cotton thread, which is slightly thicker and thus requires some adjustments to the standard long and short shaded satin stitch. The introduction and practice of the embroidery technique has made such adjustments to account for the use of cotton thread.

Embroidery Technique

1

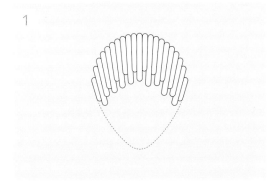

As shown in the picture, embroider the first batch along the outer contour line, where one stitch is long and the next stitch is short. The length of the short stitch is approximately three-quarters of the long stitch, but it is more flexible and casual than the regular shaded satin stitch. Generally, start embroidering from the middle of the design, making it easier to control the direction and length of the stitches.

2

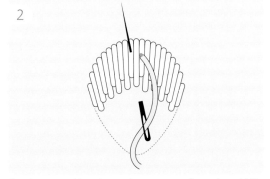

For the second batch, continue to start from the middle position. The first stitch (at the green point) should come out from approximately one-quarter or one-third of the length of the long stitch in the first batch. The second stitch should follow the direction of the silk threads in the design. The length of the stitch should be similar to the length of the long stitch in the first batch. The third stitch should come out from the fabric, with a one-thread interval between it and the first stitch.

3

Starting from the second batch, the stitches should be spaced one stitch apart, similar to the regular shaded satin stitch. Except for changes at the turning points or edges according to the pattern, the length of the stitches in the second batch should generally be the same. However, the upper and lower edges of the stitches in the second batch should present irregular variations in height, creating a sense of unevenness.

4

In the third batch, insert the needle into the gaps between the stitches of the second batch. The exit point should be approximately one-quarter or one-third of the length of the stitches in the second batch. The length of the stitches in the third batch should be similar to the second batch, and they should also exhibit the unevenness in height to create a staggered effect.

5

For the fourth batch, follow the same technique as before. Throughout the embroidery process, always pay attention to the direction of the threads. When encountering edges, adjust the length of the stitches according to the actual situation.

6

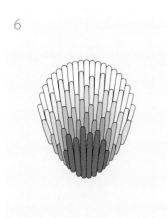

According to the pattern, embroider batch by batch as described above until the entire design is filled.

Tips

1. If silk thread is used for the embroidery of long and short shaded satin stitch, the second batch will come out at approximately one-fifth of the first batch.

2. Apart from the first batch, the thread lines of each subsequent batch should be uneven in height. In simple terms, if the exit point of a thread is high, then the entry point should also be high. Similarly, if the exit point is low, then the entry point should also be low. For long and short shaded satin stitch, the stitches of each batch are scattered and won't form neat edges like those stitches of regular shaded satin stitch. This allows for a better blending and intertwining of different colors, without creating distinct boundary lines.

3. When arranging the threads, always pay attention to changes in the direction of the threads. At turning points, it is necessary to appropriately shorten the stitches to ensure smooth and seamless transitions in each batch.

4. The long and short shaded satin stitch can be used for both complex color transitions and embroidering large areas of solid color. Unlike satin stitch technique, which is limited by stitch spacing, the long and short shaded satin stitch can be used to fill infinitely large patterns. Moreover, compared to the regular shaded satin stitch, the stitches in each batch blend more discreetly and naturally.

Embroidery Project: *Butterfly*

The symbolic significance of butterflies in traditional Chinese culture is rich and mysterious. The ancient Chinese philosopher Zhuangzi (c. 369–c. 286 BC) once dreamt of himself transforming into a colorful butterfly, freely fluttering and experiencing extreme happiness. Upon waking up, Zhuangzi couldn't help but wonder if he was originally a butterfly dreaming of being a human or a human dreaming of being a butterfly. This dream was perhaps one of the most beautiful and enigmatic in ancient China.

This artwork uses the long and short shaded satin stitch technique with blue and brown threads to depict fluttering butterflies.

Materials

Base fabric: white organza.

Embroidery threads: **OLYMPUS** No. 25 embroidery threads 745#, 744#, 743#, 2039#, 2040#, 2041#, 2042#, 3835# and 384# (single strand).

Steps

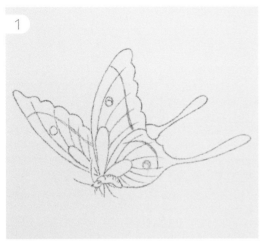

Draw the embroidery design and auxiliary lines on the base fabric using a heat erasable pen. Since the long and short shaded satin stitch is more free-form than regular shaded satin stitch or round shaded satin stitch, there is usually no need for layered auxiliary lines.

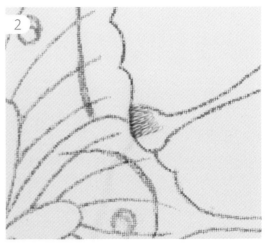

Using a single strand of thread 2042#, begin stitching from the middle of the design toward one side. Alternate between long and short stitches, with the length of the stitches varying according to the shape of the design. Generally, the short stitches should be around three-quarters or two-thirds of the length of the long stitches. Pay attention to ensure that the exit point of each stitch covers the left contour line of the design.

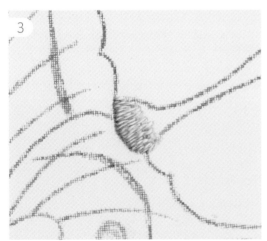

Using the same method, stitch the other half in the same manner to complete the first batch of embroidery.

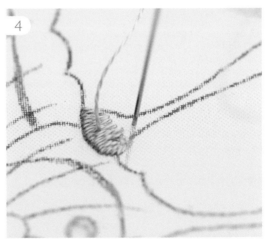

Using a single strand of thread 2041#, begin stitching the second batch from the middle, as before. The exit points of the stitches should be approximately one-fourth to one-third of the length of the long stitches in the first batch, typically between two long stitches of the first batch. Stitch in the direction of the thread grain and maintain a spacing between the exit and entry points similar to the length of the long stitches in the middle of the first batch.

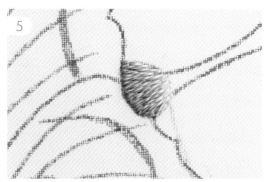

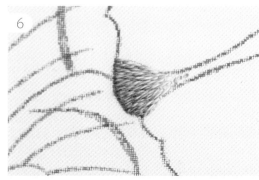

In the second batch, the stitches should be inserted mostly between the long stitches of the first batch. However, the exit points should vary in height, resulting in uneven entry points. Stitch one side first, then the other side to complete the second batch. The key is to avoid creating a consistent curve with the second batch of stitches. Instead, they should naturally intertwine and blend with the first batch, creating a scattered, intertwining effect.

Continue using a single strand of thread 2041# to stitch the third batch. In the third batch, the stitches should be inserted mostly between the two stitches of the second batch. The exit points should be approximately one-fourth to one-third of the length of the stitches of the second batch. The stitching method remains the same as before. Pay attention to the changing direction of the threads near the outline as the shape narrows, and appropriately reduce the number of stitches to maintain a smooth transition.

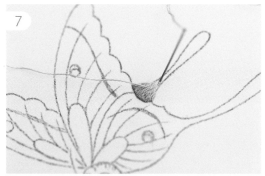

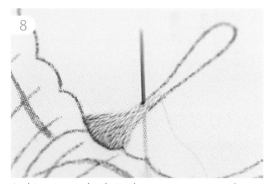

Using a single strand of thread 2040#, stitch the fourth batch from the middle toward both sides. The exit points should be approximately one-fourth to one-third of the length of the stitches in the previous batch. The length of the stitches in the middle should be similar to the length of the stitches in the middle of the previous batch.

At this point, as the design becomes narrower and elongated, you can continue using the same thread. Stitch each batch one after another using the same method. When stitching the edges, as shown in the diagram, to maintain smooth, precise outlines, you can insert the needle into the outermost stitch of the previous batch, allowing for better control of the contour lines.

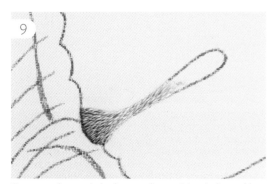

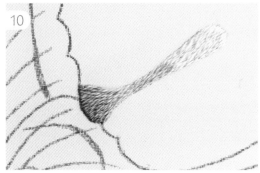

Once you have stitched up to the position indicated in the diagram using the 2040# thread, you can prepare to finish and change the thread.

Use a single strand of thread 2039# to stitch the remaining part, following the same method as before.

Next, stitch the dark edges and veins on the butterfly's wings. All the curved vein lines in the diagram will be stitched using three different colors of threads, transitioning seamlessly with the stem stitch. Start by using a single strand of thread 745# to stitch the dark edges of the butterfly's wings. Stitch until you reach the position indicated in the diagram and then stop the stitching.

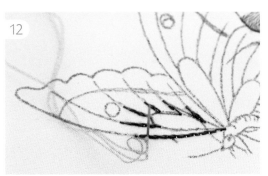

Continue using a single strand of thread 745# to stitch the five dark curved lines on the wing from the left side to the right side. The length of each stitched segment should be as shown in the diagram, approximately one-third of the curved line's length. For beginners, you can simply pull the thread to the starting point of the next curved line after completing one. After finishing the first part of the six curved segments, switch to a single strand of thread 744# to continue the stem stitch for the second segment. Please note that the exit point for the needle should be halfway between the last stitch of the 745# thread (marked with a green dot).

Using the 744# thread, continue the stem stitch, ensuring that the stitch spacing is the same as the previous stitches.

Using the 744# thread, stitch the middle section of the outermost curved line, which should be one-third of the total length. Repeat the same method to stitch the middle sections of the other five curved lines, each also being one-third of the total length.

Continue stitching from the outer side to the inner side using the 743# thread, completing the last part of the six curved lines with the stem stitch.

Start the first batch of long and short shaded satin stitches using a single strand of thread 2039# from the outer edge of the wing. Exit the needle at the top of the contour line. When inserting the needle, place it right next to the outer stem stitches.

When stitching, bring the needle out from the outer edge of the contour line, paying attention to the direction of the thread grain when inserting the needle. Alternate between long and short stitches, maintaining the same proportion as before.

Complete the first batch of stitches for this section of the wing. Be sure to skip over the previously stitched curved lines using the stem stitch, but ensure there are no gaps left between the stitches.

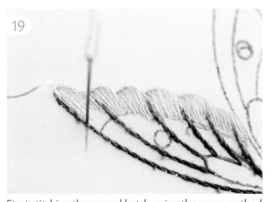

Start stitching the second batch, using the same method for inserting the needle and bringing it out as before, following the pattern of the wing's tail section.

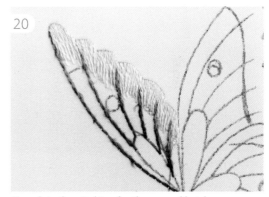

Complete the stitching for the second batch.

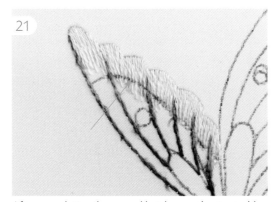

After completing the second batch, use a heat erasable pen to draw the partially covered horizontal curved lines on top of the stitched threads, as indicated by the arrow. It is important to do this touch-up work promptly. If you wait until the markings on the fabric are completely covered, it will be much more difficult to add the missing lines.

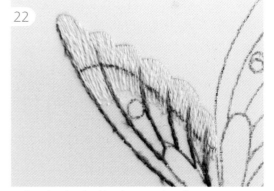

Embroider the third batch, extending the coverage area of the 2039# thread. After completing the third batch, continue to draw the missing lines that were covered by the stitches. From this point on, it is important to pay close attention to the relationship between the stitches and the brown veins. There should be no gaps between them, but at the same time, be careful not to compress the brown veins too tightly, as this can cause uneven thickness.

Use the 2040# thread to stitch two batches of lines, covering the areas as shown in the diagram.

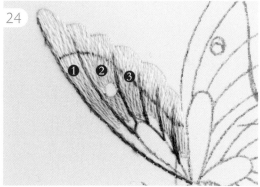

Continue stitching the long and short shaded satin stitches within the designated grids (1, 2, 3) using the 2041# single-strand thread, as shown in the diagram. Complete the stitching as depicted in the provided image. From this step onwards, the number of batches for each color will no longer be specified. You can adjust the length of the stitches according to your own preference and the desired effect.

Use the 2042# single-strand thread to complete the remaining portions within grids 1, 2, and 3. Pay attention to ensure that the stitches hold down the contour lines of the drop-shaped center of the wing.

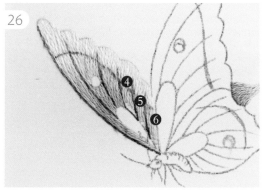

Use the 3835# single-strand thread to stitch the areas within grids 4, 5, and 6. Complete the stitching according to the image.

Use the 384# single-strand thread to complete the remaining portions within grids 4, 5, and 6.

Use the 2039# single-strand thread to stitch the drop-shaped section. You can start the stitches from the inside of the shape and tuck the needle under the tail end of previously stitched threads, which will help create precise contours.

The range stitched using the 2039# thread is as shown in the image.

Use 2040# single-strand embroidery thread to embroider the remaining parts of the teardrop shape.

Use the 745#, 744# and 743# single-strand threads to stitch the veins on the right wing. Continue using the stem stitch method, as described in steps 11–15. Stitch each vein from the base to the tip.

Use the 2039# single-strand thread to stitch the first color segment of the wing using the long and short shaded satin stitch method. Divide it into several batches, following the previous method, and complete it according to the image. When stitching, make sure to promptly use a heat erasable pen to draw the missing arc on the stitched lines.

Use the 2040# single-strand thread to stitch the second color segments, following the image to achieve the desired final result.

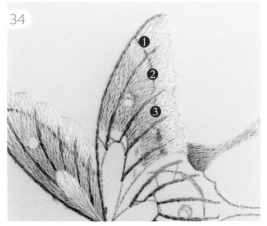

34

Use the 2041# single-strand thread to stitch the third color segments in grids 1, 2, and 3, as indicated in the image.

35

Use the 2042# single-strand thread to stitch the remaining parts in grids 1, 2, and 3, as indicated in the image.

36

Use the 3835# single-strand thread to stitch the third color segments in grids 4 and 5, as shown in the image.

37

Use the 384# single-strand thread to stitch the remaining portions inside grids 4 and 5, as shown in the image.

38

Use the 2039# single-strand thread to stitch the first color segment in the middle teardrop shaped area of the wing, as shown in the image.

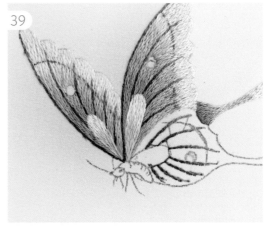

39

Use the 2040# single-strand thread to complete stitching the remaining portion of the teardrop shape.

Use the 2039# single-strand thread to stitch the tail portion of the wing using the long and short shaded satin stitch method as shown in the diagrams. Also, remember to promptly fill in any missing arcs with a pen.

Use the 2040# single-strand thread to stitch the second color segments as shown in the diagram to achieve the desired effect.

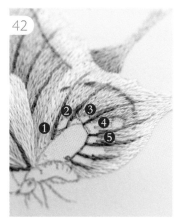

Use the 2041# single-strand thread to stitch the third color segments in grids 1, 2, 3, 4, and 5 of the wing, as shown in the diagram, to achieve the desired effect.

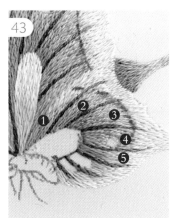

Use 2042# single-strand thread to embroider the remaining parts of grids 1, 2, 3, 4, and 5.

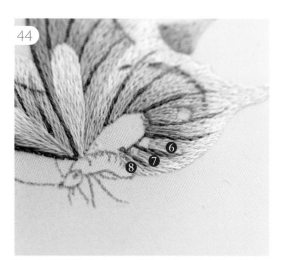

Use the 3835# single-strand thread to stitch the third color segments in grids 6, 7, and 8 of the wing to achieve the desired effect.

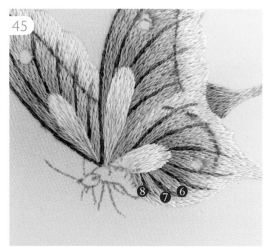

Use the 384# single-strand thread to stitch the remaining portions of grids 6, 7, and 8 of the wing. Then, use the 2039# embroidery thread to stitch the first color segment of the teardrop shape in the middle of the wing. This will result in the desired effect as shown in the image.

Use the 2040# single-strand thread to stitch the remaining portion of the teardrop shape.

Embroider the curved lines on the three wings using the method of couching stitch in the gold thread couching stitch on page 141. Both the main thread in the center and the stitching thread used to secure the main thread are 744# single-strand threads, with a spacing of approximately 2 mm between each stitched thread.

Use a heat erasable pen to clearly outline the three circular contours on the wings and indicate the approximate boundaries of the first layer's color.

The circular patterns are embroidered using the basic encroaching satin stitch method. First, use 745# single-strand thread to stitch the first layer of color for the circles.

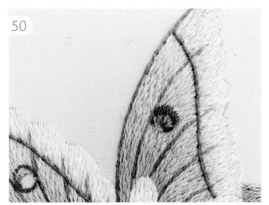

Stitch the second layer of color for the circles using 743# single-strand embroidery thread.

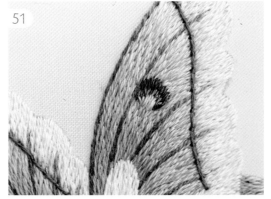

Use 2039# single-strand thread to complete the remaining part of the circle. At this point, the embroidery thread is already quite thick, and the stitches are very short, so it is not necessary to strive for perfect contours.

Embroider the remaining two circles using the same method.

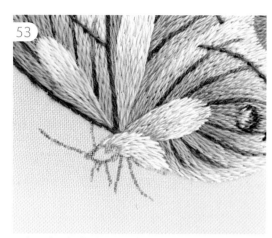

Embroider the body part of the butterfly using 2039# single-strand thread, using regular shaded satin stitch technique.

Add a few stitches to the tail, abdomen, and back of the body using 743# single-strand thread to enhance the color gradient and create a sense of fuzziness on the butterfly's body.

Embroider the whiskers and legs using 745# single-strand thread. For longer lines, you can use the stem stitch, while shorter lines can be done with simple short stitches.

Embroider the head using 745# embroidery thread. Use the first batch of stitches in the long and short shaded satin stitch technique.

Use 745# single-strand thread to make two loops of knot stitches to complete the butterfly's eyes. The artwork is now finished.

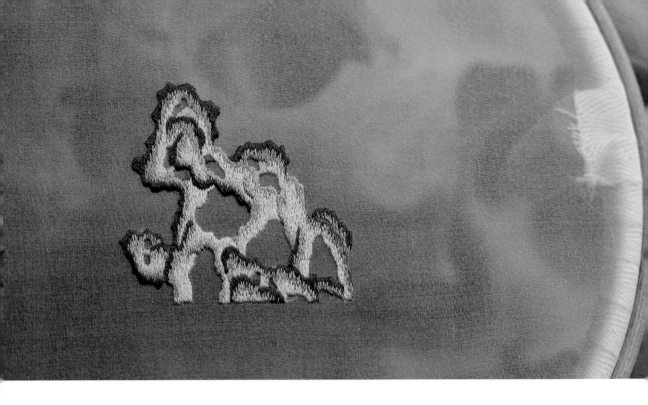

12. Blended Stitch (Long and Short Stitch)

The basic characteristics of blended stitch in traditional Chinese needlework are similar to the long and short stitch of European or American embroidery. It is an embroidery technique that use varied lengths of stitches to create a more free-form design with intermingling lines. Compared to long and short shaded satin stitch, the technique of blended

Fig. 60 Embroidery of *Farming and Weaving* of Qing Dynasty
The embroidery artwork is exquisite in its craftsmanship, and the head of the cow is created using blended stitch, as shown in the detail image on the left.

stitch results in more obvious stitches and a slightly less natural blending of colors. However, when portraying significant color variations, blended stitch offers greater freedom and achieves better effects. In traditional Chinese embroidery, blended stitch is often combined with many other stitching techniques to achieve a more convenient, flexible way of depicting the embroidered subject (fig. 60).

Embroidery Technique

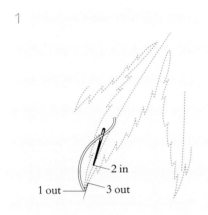

The diagram illustrates the embroidery technique using a leaf as an example. The first stitch starts from the tip of the leaf's outline, bringing the needle out, and the second stitch goes into the needlework on the midrib of the leaf, with the stitch distance not exceeding 8 mm. The specific length depends on the direction of the midrib. The third stitch comes out from the right side of the leaf's outline, leaving an appropriate distance from the first stitch.

The first batch of threads is arranged along the outer contour line, with varying lengths for each thread segment. Usually, the first batch of threads is stitched along the outer contour line in a staggered manner, with irregular entry points on the inner side, so that the stitches can have alternating lengths, with some longer and others shorter. Alternatively, as shown in the diagram, they can be arranged in a more varied, artistic way, creating a richer, more diverse pattern.

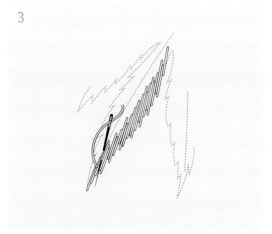

When embroidering the second batch of threads, you can bring the needle out from between the two threads of the first batch, as shown in the diagram. Additionally, the points where the needle comes out should also be varied in height, creating an uneven or staggered effect.

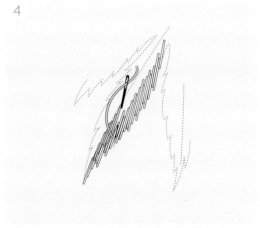

When interweaving with the first batch of threads, depending on the specific arrangement, you can also bring the needle out from the body of the first batch of threads. Blended stitch does not require every stitch to come out from the gaps of the previous batch.

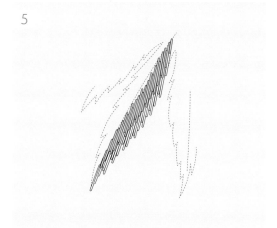

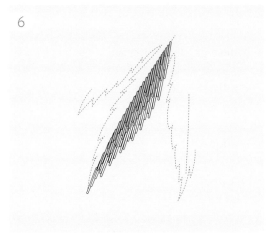

The image depicts the state of the piece after completing the second batch of stitches.

The third batch of stitches follows the same method as the second set. The points where the stitches come out blend with the second set in varied heights, creating an uneven, staggered appearance. However, for the entry points, the stitches should follow along the midrib of the leaf. Upon completion, the final effect will be as shown in the diagram.

Tips

1. The first batch of stitches for both blended stitch and long and short shaded satin stitch follows the same technique. The difference lies in the approach from the second set onwards. In blended stitch, you do not alternate the stitches with gaps like you do with long and short shaded satin stitch. Instead, the entire second batch is worked closely together, one stitch after the other, while ensuring that the threads' arrangements are staggered.

2. Blended stitch offers more artistic freedom, and there are no strict rules regarding how deep the stitches of the later batch should be inserted into the previous set. The depth of insertion is typically determined based on the actual design of the pattern. However, as a general guideline, when space allows, the stitches of the later batch are often inserted approximately halfway into the stitches of the previous batch.

3. The optimal length for the stitches in blended stitch embroidery is generally recommended not to exceed 8 mm. When space allows, a stitch length of 6–8 mm is considered relatively smooth and comfortable. However, if the design is intricate or the available space is limited, the stitch length may need to be shortened to accommodate the requirements of blended stitch.

4. For blending different colors of threads in the same section, beginners might prefer to frequently switch threads and embroider according to the order of the arrangement. More experienced embroiderers may choose to complete one color blending before moving on to the next color.

Embroidery Project: *Taihu Stone*

The Taihu stone is an ornamental stone commonly found in classical Chinese gardens, formed over time by the water's constant washing and erosion in rivers and lakes. The stones come in various shapes and poses, each displaying unique characteristics. This piece utilizes three traditional shades of blue in its color scheme. Blended stitch is employed to depict the interweaving of these three colors, showcasing the expressive freedom of this technique.

Materials

Base fabric: white organza.
Embroidery threads: **OLYMPUS** No. 25 embroidery thread 303# (single strand); **ANCHOR** No. 25 embroidery threads 164#, 162#, 161# and 159# (single strand).

Steps

Trace the embroidery design onto the fabric using a heat erasable pen. The dashed lines in the image represent the approximate boundaries between the three colors on the stone. When embroidering, these lines can be used as a reference to separate the colors. When embroidering this pattern, it is essential to understand the spatial arrangement of the stone and pay attention to the fact that all solid lines represent the outline of the stone. The dashed lines indicate the internal boundaries between colors. When embroidering, it is generally advisable to start by stitching the stones that are partially obscured by other elements in the design, then proceed to embroider the stones in the foreground.

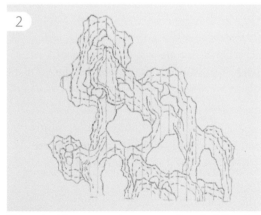

This embroidery pattern has an overall vertical direction for the stitches. It is advisable to draw vertical auxiliary lines on the fabric before starting the embroidery.

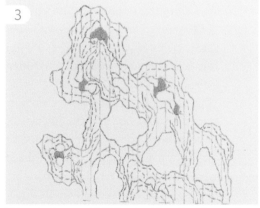

Using single-strand 303# embroidery thread, complete the sections shown in the image using the vertical satin stitch technique. Take note when encountering areas where the design connects with adjacent elements, and be sure to cover the shared outline of both patterns while embroidering.

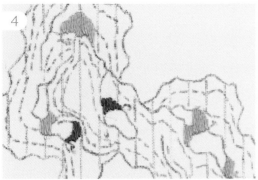

4

Using single-strand 162# embroidery thread, complete the sections shown in the image using the vertical satin stitch technique. Remember to follow the same instructions as in step 3.

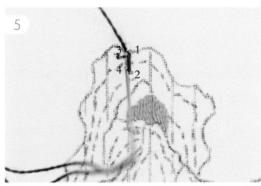

5

Start embroidering from the highest point of the Taihu stone using 164# single-strand embroidery thread. For the first stitch, bring the needle out from the contour line at the indicated position. For the second, insert the needle between the two auxiliary lines. The third stitch should be placed beside the first, coming out from the contour line. Finally, the fourth stitch should be inserted slightly higher than the second, forming one longer stitch and one slightly shorter stitch. Please note that in blended stitch embroidery, the auxiliary lines indicating color boundaries should be treated as a reference only. Unlike regular shaded satin stitch or basic encroaching satin stitch techniques, blended stitch does not create clear, distinct boundaries between colors. Generally, the stitches of the first batch should extend beyond the first layer of color boundary. When blending the second batch of stitches into the first, they should be positioned higher than the color boundary so that the staggered, interwoven positions of the two colors will roughly correspond to the locations of the auxiliary line.

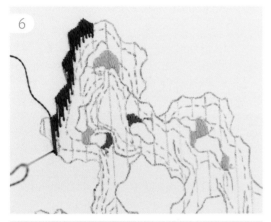

6

When embroidering the first batch of stitches, pay attention to the accuracy and delicacy of the outer contour lines, while also ensuring that the internal stitching points vary in height. When encountering a situation as shown in the image, you can fill the protruding part on the left side of the last long stitch using vertical satin stitches, as shown in the upper image.

Embroider the first batch of stitches as shown in the lower image.

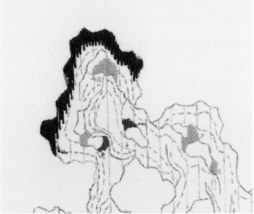

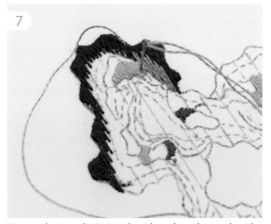

7

Use single-strand 161# embroidery thread to embroider the second color of the pattern. When embroidering the second batch, make sure to vary the heights of the stitches at both the entry and exit points, placing one stitch immediately after the other. The depth at which the second color is blended into the first color depends on how much of the deep blue shape you wish to retain. Since the first auxiliary line has been covered by stitches, when embroidering the second color, you can refer to the pattern or flexibly adjust based on the colors of the first layer.

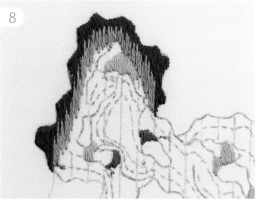

When encountering the edge lines while embroidering, simply follow along the edge and insert the needle accordingly. Continue stitching the second batch until you reach the left side.

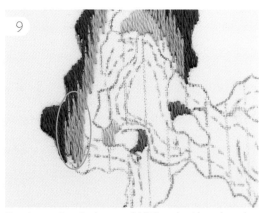

Continue using single-strand 161# embroidery thread to embroider another batch after the leftmost part of the second batch, extending the sky blue color further (indicated by the circle) as shown in the image.

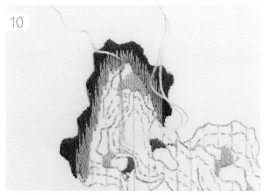

Begin embroidering the third layer using single-strand 159# embroidery thread, starting from the indicated position as shown in the image.

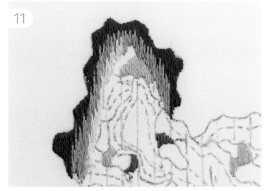

Continue embroidering to the left, following the same method as the second layer, until you reach the far-left side. When embroidering this batch, you do not need to specifically ensure that every stitch reaches the outer contour line. Focus on creating a visually varied effect with stitches of different lengths.

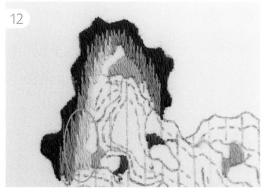

Continue using single-strand 159# embroidery thread to pick up where you left off with the previous batch and embroider with the light blue color until you reach the contour edge. Then, fill the remaining section on the bottom left side, extending it toward the right (as shown in the circle).

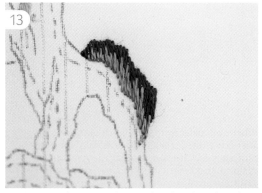

Use 164# and 161# single-strand embroidery threads to sequentially embroider the first and second batches of the protruding stone on the far right of the pattern.

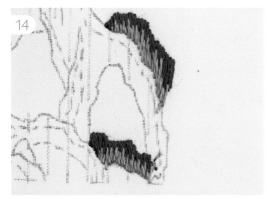

14

Use 164# and 161# single-strand embroidery threads to embroider the first and second batches on the stone in the bottom right corner of the pattern. When stitching the second batch, make sure that the entry points of the stitches cover the outline of the previous stone.

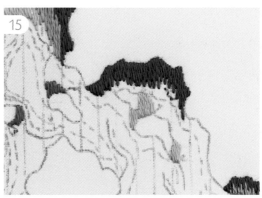

15

Use single-strand 164# embroidery thread to embroider the first batch for the protruding stone at the indicated position as shown in the image.

16

Use single-strand 161# embroidery thread to continue from the previous section of deep blue color and extend it to the stone below. When stitching this section, at the point where it meets the already embroidered 303# thread (indicated by the red mark), pass the needle through the 303# thread to ensure that the edge where they connect remains seamless and no white gaps are visible.

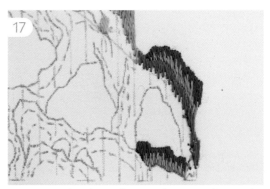

17

Continue embroidering downward using single-strand 162# embroidery thread, connecting to the portion previously embroidered with 161# thread in step 14. Since this section of 162# thread needs to cover the second section (161# thread) of the stone behind it, you can use a technique of bringing the needle out from the inside and inserting it towards the edge. This method allows for more precise control of the edge line.

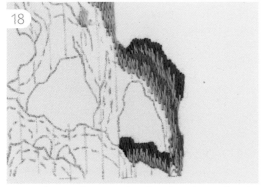

18

Use single-strand 161# embroidery thread to embroider the second batch of stitches for this section of the stone.

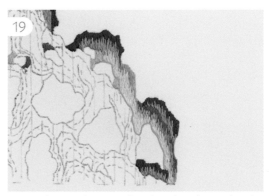

19

Use single-strand 159# embroidery thread to embroider the light blue color from top to bottom in one or two batches (along the green line marking), until you achieve the effect shown in the image.

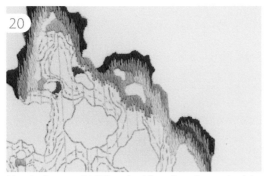

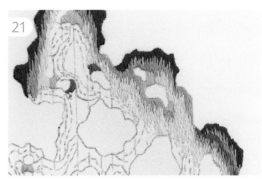

Use single-strand 161# embroidery thread to embroider the first batch of stitches for the stone in the middle part, as shown in the image.

Continue embroidering downward using single-strand 159# embroidery thread. Depending on the actual design, embroider 2–3 batches of stitches until you achieve the desired effect as shown in the image.

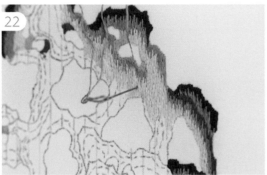

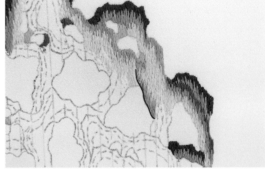

Use single-strand 161# embroidery thread to bring the needle out from the indicated position as shown in the image. Then, embroider downward along the red marking in the right image, creating a section of sky-blue color.

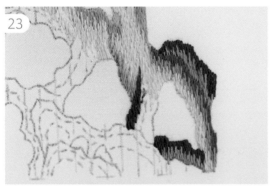

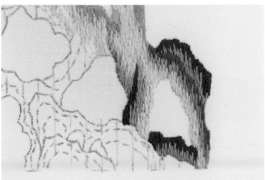

Continue embroidering downward using 164#, 161# and 159# single-strand embroidery threads, in that order, to stitch the first, second, and third batches of the stone.

Use single-strand 164# embroidery thread to embroider the first batch of stitches for the stone in the upper left corner.

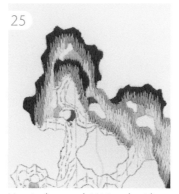

Use single-strand 161# embroidery thread to embroider the second batch of stitches and extend it toward the bottom right direction.

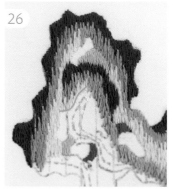

Use single-strand 159# embroidery thread to embroider a small section of light blue color on the left side (as indicated above the green marking line).

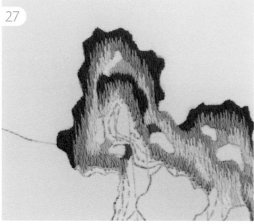

Use single-strand 161# embroidery thread to embroider the section indicated in the image (above the green marking line).

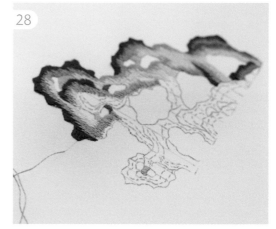

As the embroidery continues, there will be sections of the stone that require frequent thread changes. You can pass the temporarily unused embroidery threads from the underside of the fabric through the blank areas of the pattern to the top side and leave them aside for later use so that you won't need to cut and tie off the thread each time.

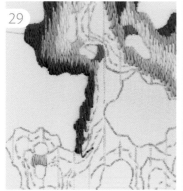

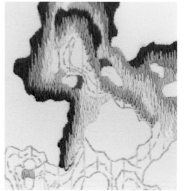

Continue embroidering from left to right using 164#, 161# and 159# single-strand embroidery threads, in that order, to stitch the first, second, and third batches of the stones.

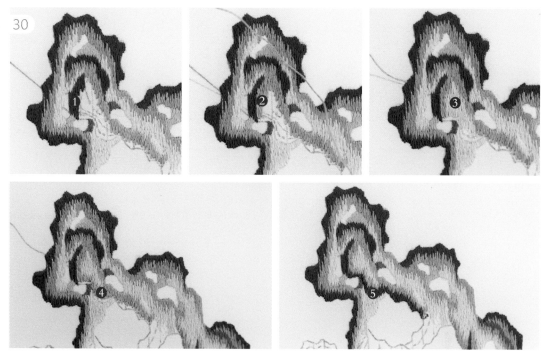

Returning to the upper half of the Taihu stone, use 164#, 161# and 159# single-strand embroidery threads to complete this section in batches, as indicated with numbers of 1 to 5 in the images.

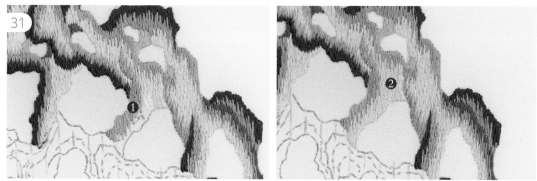

Continue embroidering downward using 161# and 159# single-strand embroidery threads, in that order, to stitch the first and second batches of the stones (as shown with the numbers in the images).

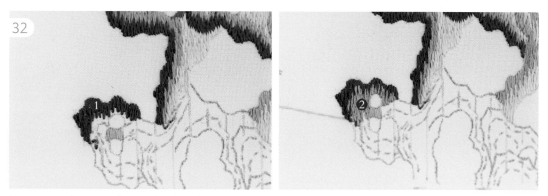

Use 164# and 161# single-strand embroidery threads to embroider the first and second batches of the protruding stone in the bottom left corner of the pattern.

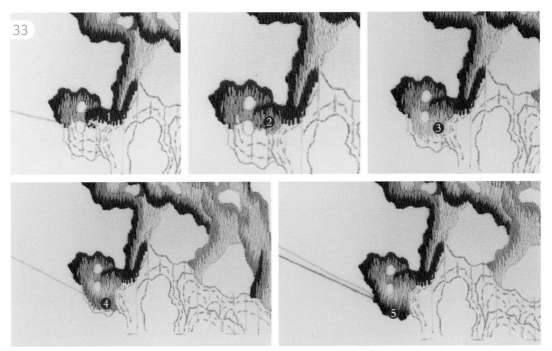

Continue embroidering downward using 164#, 161# and 159# single-strand embroidery threads to complete the embroidery of 5 parts in this section of stones.

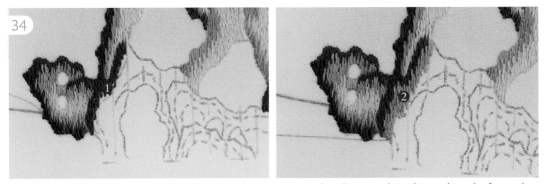

Use 164# and 161# single-strand embroidery threads to continue embroidering to the right, stitching the first and second batches of stitches for the next stone.

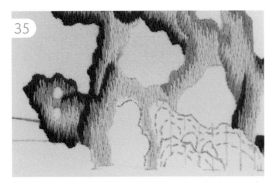

Continue embroidering to the right using single-strand 159# embroidery thread for the light blue section of the stone. Since it covers a large area, it needs to be stitched in batches.

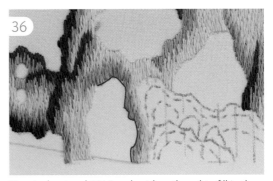

Use single-strand 161# embroidery thread to fill in the edge part of the stone along the red marking line.

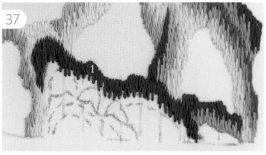

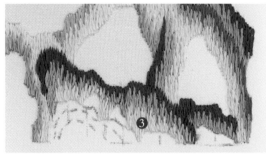

Continue using 164#, 161# and 159# single-strand embroidery threads to embroider the first, second, and third batches of stitches for the stone on the right side.

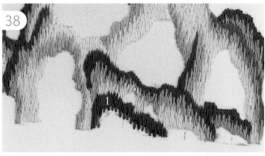

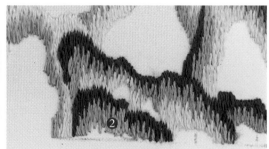

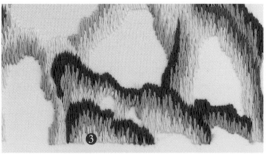

Use 164#, 161# and 159# single-strand embroidery threads to embroider the first, second, and third batches of stitches for the last stone.

The image depicts the completed embroidery.

13. Gold Thread Couching Stitch

Gold thread couching stitch has already been a mature technique during the Tang dynasty in China (fig. 61). The key of gold thread couching stitch embroidery lies in the production of gold thread. Handcrafted gold thread is created by pounding pure gold into extremely thin gold foils, which are then cut into narrow strips. These strips are affixed to paper to form gold leaf, which is polished to a glossy finish. The gold leaf is then cut into fine pieces and twisted around silk threads to create gold thread.

The stitching technique used in gold thread couching stitch embroidery is similar to that of couching stitch in Western embroidery. The use of gold thread as the main material for embroidery results in an exceptionally magnificent effect. Gold thread couching stitch is commonly used to depict the outline of patterns and can be used independently or to embellish the edges of silk thread embroidery patterns.

Fig. 61 Embroidery of Cranes and Auspicious Clouds

In the image, it can be observed that the contour of the cranes features the use of gold thread couching stitch.

Embroidery Technique

1

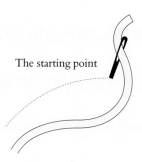

The starting point

Starting stitch: Take a thicker needle and thread it with gold thread. Insert the needle into the starting point of the pattern to secure the thread.

2

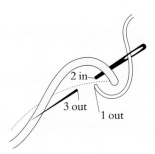

2 in
3 out
1 out

Using No. 25 embroidery thread, perform the gold thread couching stitch technique. The first stitch goes out from one side of the gold thread, and the second stitch crosses over the gold thread and goes in from the other side. The distance between the entry and exit points of the first and second stitches should be smaller than the width of the gold thread. The third stitch is made on the same side as the first stitch, at a distance of approximately 2–3 mm from the first stitch.

3

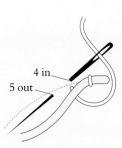

4 in
5 out

The fourth stitch crosses over the gold thread and goes in from the opposite side of the third stitch, and the fifth stitch moves forward again by 2–3 mm, going out from the same side as the first and third stitches. Repeat this pattern to complete the entire row of stitching over the gold thread.

4

When the overall stitching over the gold thread is complete, thread the tail end of the gold thread into a thicker needle and bring it through the fabric at the end of the pattern.

Tips

1. Pay attention to maintaining smooth, even gold thread during the process of the embroidery.
2. When using No. 25 embroidery thread for stitching over the gold thread, ensure that the width of the stitch does not exceed the width of the gold thread.
3. Adjust the density of the stitch based on the curvature of the design. The smaller the curvature, the higher the density of the stitch should be.

Embroidery Project: *Fortune Bat*

In Chinese culture, the character for "bat" (蝠, fú) sounds similar to the character for "fortune" (福, fú). Bats are thus often used in traditional Chinese patterns as auspicious symbols and are widely applied in various aspects of daily life, such as New Year paintings, clothing, jade ornaments and lacquerware. This small gold thread couching stitch embroidery artwork with bats as the main theme, conveying the beautiful symbolism of bestowing blessings.

Materials

Base fabric: white organza.
Embroidery threads: **OLYMPUS** No. 25 embroidery thread 512# (single strand); gold embroidery thread.

Steps

Trace the embroidery pattern onto the base fabric using a heat erasable pen.

Start by embroidering the abdomen of the bat pattern. This area has gentle curves and is an easy place to start. Use single-strand embroidery thread 512#. Begin with 2–3 small, short stitches. Choose a starting point near position 1, and make both entry and exit points along the traced lines. These stitches will be covered by the gold thread later.

Take another thicker embroidery needle and thread the gold thread, leaving a thread tail of 2–3 cm. Insert the needle at the end point of the curve and bring the thread tail to the back of the fabric. Then, remove the needle.

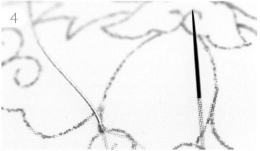

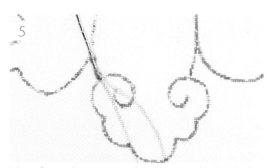

Next, use an embroidery needle threaded with the 512# embroidery thread to start the couching. When stitching, always come out from the left side of the gold thread and go in from the right side, creating one stitch per entry and exit. The first and second stitches should be made right next to the point where the gold thread meets the fabric to secure it. Make sure both the entry and exit points are along the traced lines to ensure the gold thread remains straight and the stitches are not spaced too far apart.

Move forward approximately 2 mm to make the third stitch. Again, come out from the left side and go in from the right side, ensuring that the points of entry and exit are on the marked line. Each stitch should be gently pulled tight, while also keeping the stitched gold thread smooth and even.

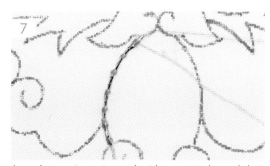

Continue stitching using the same method until you reach near the end of this line segment. When there is approximately 2–3 mm left to the end, cut the gold thread. For beginners, it may be helpful to leave a slightly longer length of gold thread (5–8 cm) for easier threading, while more experienced individuals can leave it shorter (3–4 cm). Thread the end of the gold thread through a thicker embroidery needle and insert the needle at the endpoint of the line, pulling the gold thread to the back of the fabric.

As at the starting point, embroider two stitches tightly next to the end of the thread to secure the gold thread.

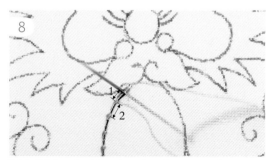

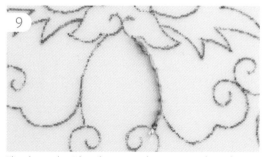

With 512# embroidery thread, make two starting stitches at the locations covered by the gold thread. When stitching, make sure to angle the needle diagonally between the gold thread and the fabric to avoid damaging the gold thread. You can make the two starting stitches, at positions 1 and 2.

Flip the embroidered piece to the reverse side and trim the ends of the gold thread, leaving approximately 1 mm.

10

Embroider the curve on the opposite side using the same method.

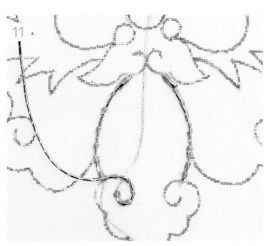

11

Begin embroidering the tail using the same starting method as before. However, since this section of the curve has smaller curvature, adjust the spacing between stitches to make them closer together.

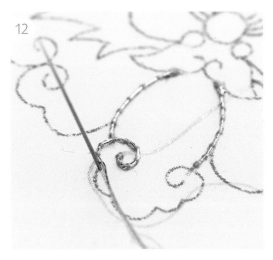

12

When encountering inward concave corners, make sure to stitch at the pointed area marked on the fabric. This will create sharper corners. After stitching the corner, use your hand to pull the embroidery thread tightly from the back of the fabric while bending the gold thread in the direction you will continue stitching. You can use your fingernail to slightly pinch and assist in shaping the thread. Then, continue stitching.

13

Complete the stitching of the tail.

14

Complete the embroidery of a portion of the wings on both sides of the abdomen.

15

In order to minimize thread breaks in the gold thread couching stitch, you can embroider the head curve together with the curve of the eyes and the outer edge of the wings. Pay attention to making a couching stitch at the intersection point (the green dot) in the right picture to ensure accuracy of the shape.

16

When reaching the end of the outer curve of the wing, you can cut the gold thread, leaving it with a length of 10–15 cm, and use a thick needle to guide the gold thread to the back of the fabric.

17

Guide the gold thread out from the endpoint of the adjacent inner curve of the wing. This avoids the need for an additional start and finish. Be careful to pull the gold thread through the needle hole in a way that keeps it centered and avoids scraping the edges of the hole against the gold thread.

18

When two curves are close together, you can cross the stitching lines over both gold threads to secure them together. This will result in a finer overlap in the embroidery.

19

Complete the embroidery of the body.

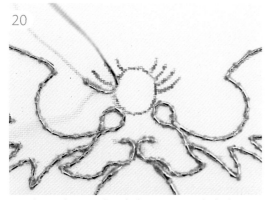

20

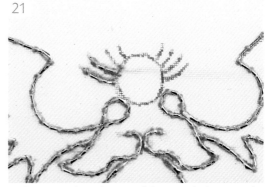

21

Start by working on the whiskers. Begin with the longest one. Cut a piece of gold thread approximately 10 cm in length and start couching from the outer endpoint towards the inner side. When you reach the inner endpoint, bring the gold thread to the back, and then bring it out from the inner endpoint of the adjacent whisker.

At the inner side endpoints of the two whiskers near the circular shape, create a stitch respectively to secure the gold thread. Continue embroidering the second whisker, then cut the thread at the back and make a finishing stitch using 512# embroidery thread at an appropriate position to handle the outer side endpoint.

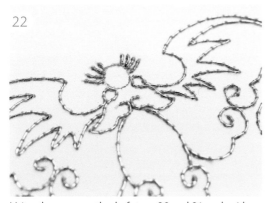

22

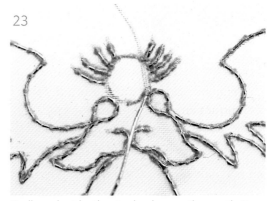

23

Using the same method of steps 20 and 21, embroider all the whiskers by stitching a segment of gold thread for every two whiskers.

Finally, embroider the circular shape as the mouth. Since a circle inevitably has a starting point and an ending point, for aesthetics, try to place the joint in a relatively concealed position, such as the overlapping area between the eyes and the mouth.

24

Complete the entire embroidery.

14. Goldwork Embroidery

The *pingjinxiu* (goldwork embroidery) and *panjinxiu* (gold thread couching stitch) techniques emerged simultaneously during the Tang dynasty and became popular in the attire of noblewomen, especially those in the imperial court (fig. 62). This popularity was closely associated with the prevailing custom and fashion of using gold in the aristocratic society of that era.

Goldwork embroidery involves filling the entire pattern with gold threads, creating a more grand, luxurious effect based on the gold thread couching stitch technique. It was later extensively used in traditional Chinese royal garments. Goldwork embroidery can be done using either double-threaded or single-threaded gold threads, although the former is more commonly employed. Here, we will use double-threaded gold threads as an example for illustration.

Fig. 62 Woman's Silk Gauze Upper Garment of Ming Dynasty
Shandong Provincial Museum
This garment displays the graceful designs of dragons and flowers using goldwork embroidery.

Embroidery Technique

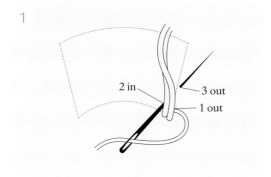

1

2 in   3 out
1 out

Take a thicker needle and thread it with two strands of gold threads. Guide the end of the gold threads to the starting point of the pattern. Use a No. 25 embroidery thread for stitching and align the outer side of the double-strand gold threads with the edge of the pattern. The first stitch is made vertically from the outer side of the gold threads, while the second stitch crosses over the gold threads and enters vertically from the other side. The distance between the exit and entry points of the first and second stitches should be the same as the width of the double-strand gold threads. The third stitch is made on the same side as the first stitch, with a spacing of approximately 2–3 mm from the first stitch.

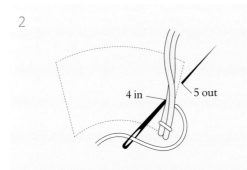

2

4 in   5 out

The fourth stitch crosses over the gold threads and enters from the opposite side of the third stitch. The fifth stitch advances another 2–3 mm, exiting on the same side as the first and third stitches.

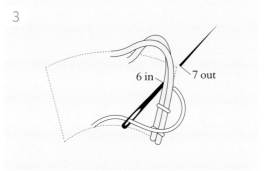

3

6 in   7 out

The sixth stitch is the same as the fourth stitch. The seventh stitch exits from the outer side of the corner of the pattern.

Tips

1. When stitching with double-strand gold threads, the needle should be perpendicular to the fabric surface, creating stitches that are the same width as the double-strand gold threads. This ensures that the stitched gold threads remain flat, straight, and evenly distributed. Stitching too narrowly can cause the threads to stack or create a segmented shrinking effect, while stitching too wide can make the stitches too prominent.
2. Be careful to maintain smooth and even gold threads in the middle of the embroidery.
3. If there is a rounded corner, it may not be necessary to stitch the double-strand gold threads separately. Depending on the situation, you can decide whether to stitch them separately or combine them.
4. When reaching the innermost circle, if there is not enough space for both strands of the gold threads, you can first bring one strand to the back of the fabric and then fill the last circle with the remaining single-strand gold thread.

4

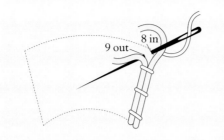

5

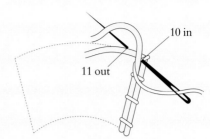

When encountering sharp corner, it is generally necessary to separate the two strands of gold threads to ensure the shape of the corner. The eighth stitch crosses over the outer gold thread and tightly stitches it upon entry. The ninth stitch should exit at a distance of one strand of gold thread from the eighth stitch. Note that the exit and entry points of the seventh, eighth, and ninth stitches should be located on the central axis of the angle at the corner.

The tenth stitch secures the inner gold thread closer to the pattern. It is important to note that the entry point of the tenth stitch is generally the same as that of the eighth stitch, also on the central axis of the angle at the corner. The eleventh stitch exits from the outer side of the gold threads, with a spacing of approximately 2–3 mm from the seventh stitch.

6

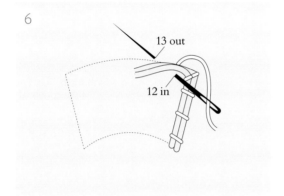

7

The twelfth and thirteenth stitches follow the same method as the fourth and fifth stitches.

Repeat the above steps until the entire pattern is filled with gold threads. When reaching the innermost circle, it is common to directly secure the double-strand gold threads with a single stitch at the turning point. Once the entire goldwork embroidery is complete, thread the end of the gold threads into a thicker needle and bring it through the fabric from the end of the pattern.

Embroidery Project: *Chinese Character of "Good Fortune"*

The character 福 (*fú*) appeared in the earliest Chinese oracle bone inscriptions. The complete character represents a jar of wine offered in front of a deity, symbolizing prayers for all things to go smoothly. Therefore, the meaning of 福 is to live a rich, fulfilling life under the blessings of the gods. Chinese people often display the character 福 during the Lunar New Year to express wishes for abundance, good health, and a smooth, peaceful life. The character 福 is also one of the most common goldwork symbols in Chinese embroidery.

Materials

Base fabric: white organza.

Embroidery threads: **OLYMPUS** No. 25 embroidery thread 512# (single strand); gold embroidery thread.

Steps

Transfer the embroidery design onto the fabric using a heat erasable pen.

Thread both strands of gold threads through a thicker embroidery needle for a short length and insert them into the back of the fabric at the indicated position as shown in the diagram. Use the 512# yellow single-strand embroidery thread and start with 2–3 small short stitches. Choose the starting point near the end where the gold threads are inserted, ensuring that both the exit and entry points are on the marked lines that will be covered by the gold threads.

Secure the double strands of gold threads by stitching two consecutive stitches at the base of the gold threads. Be sure to make these two stitches close together, with the exit points on the marked line and crossing over the double strands of gold threads before piercing closely to the exit points.

Move forward approximately 3 mm, exit the needle from the marked line, cross over the double strands of gold threads, and vertically insert the needle from the inside of the gold threads. Repeat this process to secure the gold threads, progressing toward the corner.

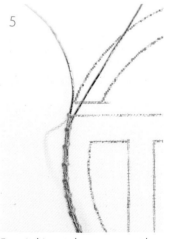

For stitching at the corner, start by securing the outer gold thread. Exit the needle from the outer edge of the marked line at the turn, cross over one strand of the gold thread, and closely insert the needle at a 45-degree angle toward the lower right direction.

6

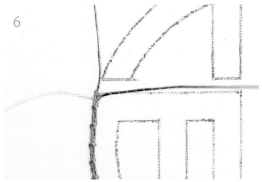

Continue to secure the inner strand of the gold threads, following the instruction outlined in step 4 of Embroidery Technique on page 149.

7

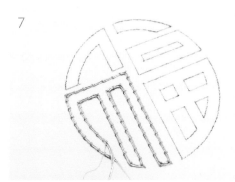

Using the same method, secure the gold threads and complete the embroidery of the outer circle until it intersects with the starting point.

8

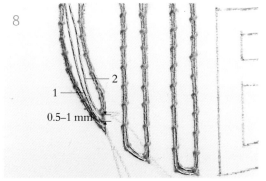

The closing point of the outer circle forms an acute angle. When securing the outer gold thread (1), it should be positioned closely to the inner side of the double strands of gold threads at the starting point of the design. While securing the other strand of gold threads (2), if it is placed too close to the outer thread, it may become cluttered and result in an unsmooth turn. Therefore, when stitching the inner gold thread (2), it is recommended that a space of 0.5–1 mm from the outer gold thread (1) be maintained to ensure that the embroidered lines at the turning point do not pile up.

9

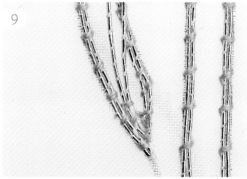

After handling the corner, continue with the second round of stitching. It is important to note that the stitches of the second round should be offset from those of the first round, with each stitch placed approximately halfway between the two stitches of the first round.

10

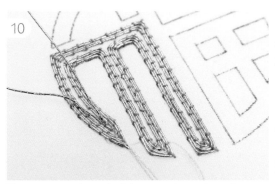

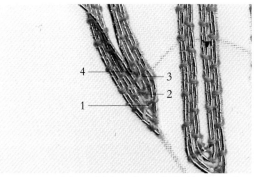

The corners at the end of the second round are sharper and narrower, and the gold threads are folded back. At this point, fold the outer gold thread back to form a double strand and secure it at the top bend of this gold thread (stitch 1). Then, cross over this double strand at the corner and secure it with a stitch (stitch 2). Moving forward, cross the double strand at the point where it is offset from the stitches of the second round (stitch 3). Bend the inner gold thread and secure it with a stitch at the top (stitch 4). After completing the turn with the two strands of gold thread, you can proceed with stitching the final round.

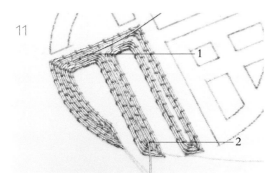

11

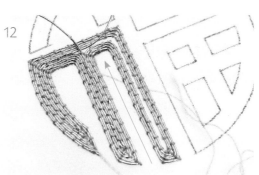

12

As shown in the diagram, the last circle only has space for the two strands of gold threads. A special technique is used when the double strands of coiled gold threads need to turn toward the vertical line in the pattern. At the turning point, first set aside the outer strand of gold threads and use only the inner strand to turn into the gap of the vertical line below. After making the first stitch at the turning point (position 1), pull the inner strand of gold threads to the top of the vertical line and secure it with a stitch at the top (position 2).

After securing the top, fold the single strand of gold thread in half to form double strands. Use the stitch method to secure these double strands of gold threads from the top to the horizontal line (see the arrow), where they meet with the other strand of gold threads that was set aside earlier.

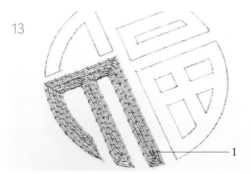

13

14

After the two strands of gold threads converge, continue along the remaining gap and secure them with stitches until the right vertical line is filled. At the top, use a thicker embroidery needle to guide the double strands of gold threads to the back of the fabric, and secure them with two stitches at the base (position 1). Use a finishing stitch to tidy up the thread. Flip to the back and trim the starting and ending double strands of gold threads, leaving approximately 1 mm.

Complete the three sections using the same method as shown in the illustration.

15

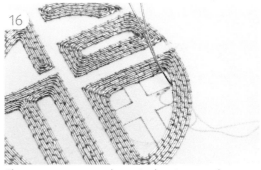

16

Divide the graphic in the bottom right corner into two parts: the outer frame of the fan shape and the cross shape. Start by embroidering the outer frame of the fan shape using the previously mentioned method.

Choose one corner as shown in the picture and start embroidering the cross shape.

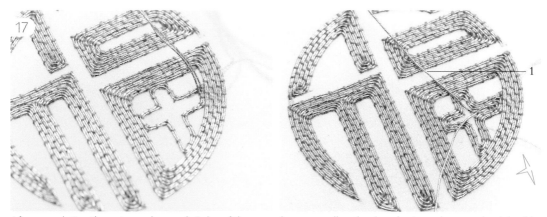

After completing the outer and second circles of the cross shape, as well as the short horizontal gap on the right side of the third circle, the remaining gaps in the upper, left, and lower directions of the pattern can be filled with only two strands of gold threads. You can use the method described in steps 10–11, where you place one strand of gold thread to the side and use only the upper strand of gold thread (strand 1) to complete the remaining work (see the marked trajectory in the image on the right).

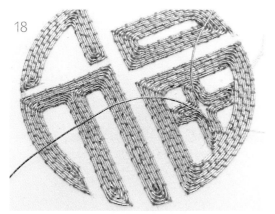

Fill the three remaining gaps using the upper strand of gold threads (strand 1 marked in step 17) and return to the center position of the cross-shaped pattern. At this point, there will be a star-shaped gap remaining at the center.

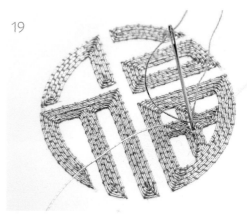

You can first leave a length of 5–6 cm for the remaining unused gold thread and then cut it. Use an embroidery needle to bring it to the back of the fabric.

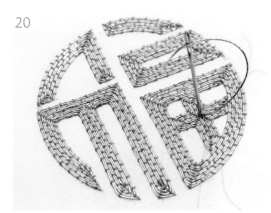

Continue filling the star-shaped gap with the remaining gold thread. After cutting it, use a needle to bring it to the back of the fabric.

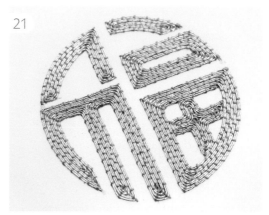

Secure the thread with a finishing stitch in a discreet location and trim the excess gold thread from the back. This completes the embroidery of the design.

15. Bead Embroidery

Bead embroidery is a technique that involves using beads as materials in embroidery. This needlework method appeared as early as the Tang dynasty, and during the Song dynasty, there were specialized practices that used a large number of pearls to embellish an embroidery. During the Northern Song dynasty (960–1127), to meet the extravagant demands of the imperial court for clothing, the government established a specialized institution known as the Embroidery Institute. Inside this institute, there were more than three hundred skilled embroiderers, and pearls became a commonly used material in embroidery (fig. 63). When applied in practice, bead embroidery techniques offer a rich variety of methods. Here, we briefly introduce three of the most basic techniques.

Fig. 63 Pearl Dragon Robe of Qing Dynasty and Its Details
The dragon robe showcases intricate bead embroidery using pearls on specific parts, with each pearl distinct and arranged in an orderly manner, making it a superb masterpiece.

Embroidery Technique

Single Bead Embroidery

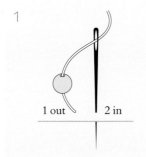

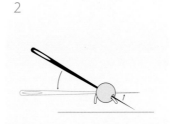

After the first stitch is taken, string the bead onto the embroidery thread. For the second stitch, the distance between the entry point and the exit point should be the same as or slightly smaller than the width of the bead.

After pulling the thread tight, the bead is fixed on the fabric. At this point, if the bead is larger and round, the hole in it may appear uneven, with one side higher than the other. To address this, as shown in the diagram, you can insert a needle into the bead hole and push the needle eye part downwards to adjust the bead hole to a horizontal position.

The image shows the finished effect of a single bead embroidery.

Spaced Bead Embroidery

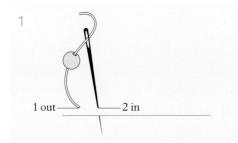

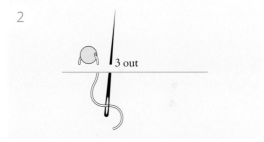

After the first stitch is taken, string the bead onto the embroidery thread. For the second stitch, the distance between the entry and exit points should be the same as the width of the bead.

According to the pattern requirements, the third stitch should begin at the position of the second bead.

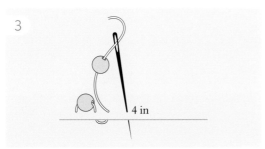

After the third stitch is made, string the bead onto the embroidery thread. The distance between the entry point of fourth stitch and exit point of third stitch should be the same as the width of the bead.

Use the same method, complete the spaced bead embroidery following the pattern requirements.

Continuous Bead Embroidery

1

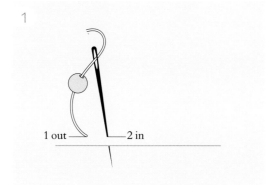

After the first stitch is made, string the bead onto the embroidery thread. The distance between the entry point of the second stitch and the exit point of the first stitch should be the same as the width of the bead.

2

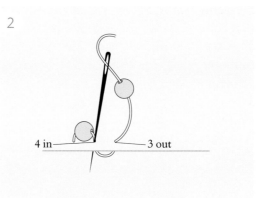

For the third stitch, the exit point should be one bead's width forward from the entry point of the second stitch. String the bead onto the embroidery thread after the third stitch. For the fourth stitch, return to the entry point of the second stitch, but it is not necessary to use the same needle hole for the entry.

3

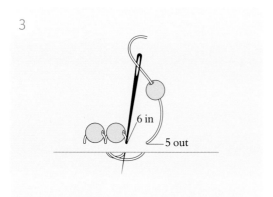

For the fifth stitch, the exit point should be one bead's width forward from the exit point of the third stitch. String the bead onto the embroidery thread after the fifth stitch. For the sixth stitch, return to the exit point of the third stitch, but it is not necessary to use the same needle hole for the entry.

4

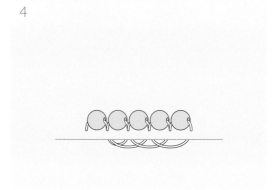

Using the same method, complete the continuous bead embroidery according to the pattern requirements.

Tips

1. If the beads being embroidered are relatively large, you can use double-strand embroidery threads or pass the needle through the bead twice when attaching each bead.
2. After completing the embroidery, it is essential to ensure that the bead holes are arranged in a horizontal direction so that they remain hidden and not visible on the surface.

Embroidery Project: *Heavenly Bamboo*

Heavenly bamboo turns red in autumn and winter, adorned with red fruits that endure, symbolizing good luck, health, longevity, and everlasting love. This artwork utilizes bead embroidery, using plump, lustrous round beads to showcase the red fruits of heavenly bamboo. This technique adds a three-dimensional effect to the flat embroidery, adding a touch of interest to the piece.

Materials

Base fabric: white organza.

Embroidery threads: **OLYMPUS** No. 25 embroidery threads 383#, 3835#, 384#, 385#, 386#, 392#, 393#, 190# (single strand); **ANCHOR** No. 25 embroidery threads 158#, 928#, 167#, 168#, 169#, 170# (single strand).

Natural coral beads: 15 beads of 6 mm in size, deep red color; 2 beads of 6 mm in size, orange color; 6 beads of 5 mm in size, orange color; 1 bead of 4 mm in size, orange color; 1 bead of 4 mm in size, deep red color.

Steps

Trace the embroidery pattern onto the fabric using a heat erasable pen.

Use single strand of 168# embroidery thread to embroider the branches of the heavenly bamboo. Make the starting stitch inside the branch and fill the branch using satin stitch method. Pay attention to the direction of the embroidery thread while stitching.

Complete the embroidery of this branch as shown in the illustration.

Use the same method to embroider the other branches in the same way.

5

Using blended (long and short) stitch method to embroider the leaves, start by embroidering the smallest leaf 1 at the bottom among the three leaves. Use single-strand embroidery thread 158# to make a starting stitch in the leaf, bring the needle out at the tip, and insert the needle along the leaf vein.

6

As shown in the diagram, during the first batch of embroidery, stitch along the edge of the leaf, ensuring the edge is neat and smooth. When stitching toward the interior of the leaf, alternate between long and short stitches to create a jagged effect, which will facilitate the insertion of the second batch of embroidery threads. Pay attention to the direction of the stitches while embroidering.

7

Use 928# embroidery thread to embroider the second layer of the leaves.

8

Fill both sides of the leaves with a scattered arrangement of long and short stitches, leaving a narrow gap in the middle for the leaf vein.

9

Use single-strand 168# embroidery thread and embroider the leaf vein using the slanted stem stitch technique.

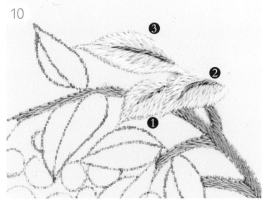

10

Repeat steps 5 to 9, embroidering leaves 2 and 3. Use single-strand 383# embroidery thread for the outer layers of the leaves, 3835# for the inner layers and 385# embroidery thread for the leaf veins.

11

Use single-strand 167# embroidery thread to embroider the outer layer of leaf 4, following the same method as the previous leaves. This leaf is larger with a full curve, so when aligning the stitches, be sure to handle the changes in the thread direction gently and smoothly.

12

Use single-strand 168# embroidery thread to embroider the inner layer of leaf 4. When the interior space of the leaf is larger, you can create a richer, more varied effect by using a scattered arrangement of long and short stitches.

13

Use single-strand 1158# embroidery thread to embroider the vein of leaf 4. Pay attention to reflecting the significant variation in thickness from the tip to the root of this vein when using the slanted stem stitch technique.

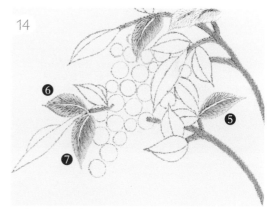

14

Embroider the leaves 5, 6 and 7 using the same color and method as described in steps 11 to 13.

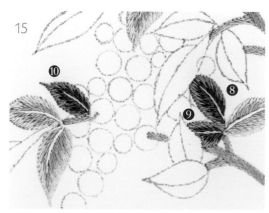

15

Repeat steps 5 to 9 and use the same method to embroider leaves 8, 9 and 10. For the outer layers, use single-strand 392# embroidery thread. For the inner layers, use single-strand 170# embroidery thread. For the leaf veins, use 384# embroidery thread.

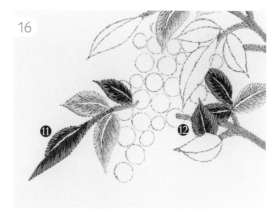

16

Repeat steps 5 to 9 using the same method to embroider leaves 11 and 12. For the outer layers, use single-strand 392# embroidery thread. For the inner layers, use single-strand 393# embroidery thread. For the leaf veins, use 384# embroidery thread.

17

Repeat steps 5 to 9, using the same method and colors to embroider leaf 13.

18

Repeat steps 5 to 9 using the same method to embroider leaves 14 and 15. For the outer layers, use single-strand 385# embroidery thread. For the inner layers, use single-strand 386# embroidery thread. For the leaf veins, use 384# embroidery thread.

19

Repeat steps 5 to 9, using the same method to embroider leaves 16 and 17. For the outer layers, use single-strand 168# embroidery thread. For the inner layers, use single-strand 169# embroidery thread. For the leaf veins, use 384# embroidery thread.

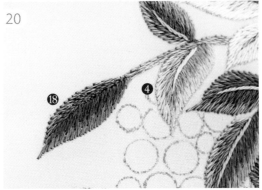

20

Repeat steps 5 to 9, using the same method to embroider leaf 18. For the outer layer, use single-strand 385# embroidery thread. For the inner layer, use single-strand 386# embroidery thread. For the leaf vein, use 384# embroidery thread.

21

Use single-strand 190# embroidery thread for bead embroidery. The beads used are 6 mm, 5 mm, and 4 mm in size in shades of deep red and orange natural coral beads and stone beads. The natural beads themselves may have color variations, which will add richness to the embroidered piece. Start by making a starting stitch at the position of the first bead and the needle comes out from the edge of the circular bead pattern.

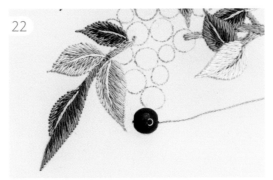

22

Choose a 6 mm bead and pass the needle through the center hole of the bead. From the exit point, insert the needle on the opposite side along the outline of the bead. After entering the needle, pull the thread tight, and then pass the needle through the center hole of the bead to adjust the orientation of the center hole to be horizontal.

23

Using the same method, attach the second 6 mm bead. Pay attention to selecting the exit point based on whether the embroidery thread beneath the fabric can be hidden well.

24

When embroidering beads, there is no specific order that must be followed. The key is to ensure that the embroidery thread on the back of the fabric is well hidden and not visible from the front. Additionally, pay attention to selecting beads of appropriate size and color.

25

The color of the beads should not be too bright or overwhelming. Generally, smaller beads and those closer to the upper part of the design can be selected in shades of orange. After attaching all the beads, make a finishing stitch under the belly of the last bead to secure and finish the embroidery. Pay attention to the numbers and their colors marked in the above diagram. The numbers represent the beads' diameter. If the number is shown in green, the bead should be in deep red. If the number is shown in blue, the bead should be in orange.

26

The image shows the finished result of the piece.

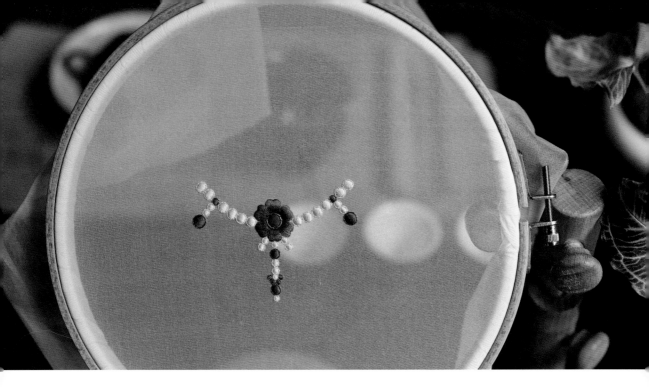

16. Padded Satin Stitch

Padded embroidery is a stitching technique that creates a raised effect on certain parts of the embroidered surface, giving a three-dimensional appearance and making the design more lifelike. It is widely used in Guangdong, or Yue embroidery, which is one of the four famous embroidery styles in China, as well as in embroidery from the Chaozhou region (fig. 64). For example, when embroidering a tree trunk, to showcase the contrast of light and shadow, one side of the tree trunk may be padded with thicker embroidery thread. Guangzhou and Chaozhou were significant regions for exporting embroidery in ancient China. Their gold and silver thread embroidery and padded embroidery were widely popular abroad.

Fig. 64 Grasshopper Pattern Pouch of Qing Dynasty
The central design of the pouch, featuring the grasshopper pattern, is created using padded embroidery, symbolizing prosperity for future generations.

The technique of padded embroidery offers a wide range of possibilities. It can be done using embroidery threads for padding or using cotton for padding. Now, more convenient and user-friendly materials such as non-woven fabric or cloth have become available. They can be used as a substitute for embroidery threads or cotton when doing padded embroidery for relatively thin or large areas. This book mainly focuses on the method of using embroidery threads for padding, which is suitable for creating raised effects in smaller and more delicate areas of embroidery.

Embroidery Technique

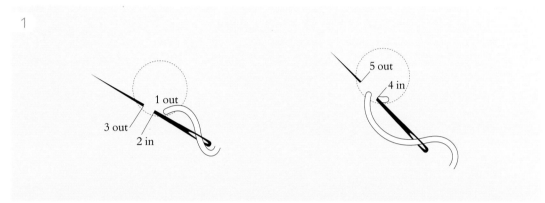

First, embroider a circle of stitches along the outline of the pattern. Use the backstitch technique, but the stitch spacing should be slightly larger than that used for the backstitch. When pulling out the needle on the inside of the outline, make sure the entry and exit points are as close to the outline as possible, but avoid stitching directly on the outline. The spacing between the exit point of the first stitch and the entry point of the second stitch is determined based on the shape of the outline. If the outline is sharply curved, the stitch spacing should be shorter. If the outline is more relaxed and straight, the stitch spacing can be slightly longer, but generally, it is kept at around 2–3 mm. The distance for the exit point of the third stitch should be the same as the spacing between the first and second stitches.

The fourth stitch should enter at the entry point of the second stitch. The distance between the exit point of the fifth stitch and the exit point of the third stitch should be the same as the spacing between the first and second stitches.

Complete the entire circle of the outline using the same method.

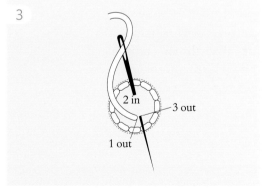

For the central padded area, create two layers of satin stitches. The first layer should be smaller, and the second layer should be larger. When embroidering the first layer, leave enough space for the second layer and a full circle of backstitch. Start the first layer by bringing the needle out from the center and embroidering satin stitches towards the right side.

4

After finishing the stitches on the right side, embroider the left side to complete the first layer of satin stitches.

5

The second layer of satin stitches should be interlocked with the first layer, and you should bring the needle in and out between the first layer of satin stitches and the outline of the backstitch. Embroider the second layer using the same satin stitch technique. Similarly, start from the center and complete one side before embroidering the other side.

6

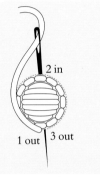

2 in

1 out　3 out

Use satin stitches to embroider the outermost layer. Start from the central axis as a reference point, making sure the entry and exit points of the stitch are along the drawn outline. The satin stitches of the outermost layer should be interlocked with the layer below it.

7

The finished effect looks like the image shown.

Tips

1. When using embroidery thread for padded satin stitch, the number of layers for padding is determined based on the size of the design and the desired raised effect. You can choose to do a single layer of padding, or you can use multiple layers. The more layers you add, the higher the raised effect will be.

2. The thread used for padding can be a single strand or multiple strands. The more strands used, the higher the raised effect will be. The number of strands should be chosen according to the desired raised effect.

3. Each layer of padded satin stitch should be interlocked, and the thread direction should vary. Based on the thread direction of the surface layer and the expected number of padding layers, one can infer the thread direction for the lowest layer of the stitches.

4. While the outline in the embroidery technique above is shown using the backstitch, in practice, you can choose different linear stitching techniques such as the stem stitch, or other appropriate stitches based on the design's needs and size.

Embroidery Project: *Pearl and Jade Necklace*

The pearl and jade necklace is a type of ornament worn on the head, neck, chest, arms, and calves, composed of flowers or precious stones. In ancient India, this type of decoration was also commonly used on Buddha statues. Later, it was introduced to China with Buddhism and became popular during the Tang dynasty, where it was imitated and improved upon. This small embroidery piece, draws its inspiration from the necklace depicted on the chest of Bodhisattvas in Buddhist paintings. It was re-designed and adapted into a smaller format, using padded satin stitch to create a three-dimensional effect for the beads of the necklace, which is very fitting.

Materials

Base fabric: white organza.
Embroidery threads: **OLYMPUS** No. 25 embroidery threads 713#, 714#, 190#, 430#, 257# (single strand); **DMC** metallic embroidery threads E301#, E3747#, E699# (single strand).

Steps

Trace the embroidery pattern onto the white organza fabric using a heat erasable pen.

Use the 190# double-strand embroidery threads to create a starting stitch at the center of the circle. Then, use the backstitch technique to embroider along the outline of the design. Since the drawn lines have a certain thickness, make sure to bring the needle in and out along the inside of the outlined contour while embroidering.

After finishing the outline, pay attention to keeping the stitches neat and not too large. The completed outline should form a circular shape.

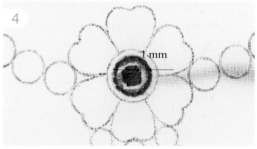

Embroider horizontal satin stitches in the central part of the circle, leaving about 1 mm between the backstitch outline and the second layer of satin stitches. While embroidering, start from the center and work toward both sides, creating a roughly circular shape. However, it is not necessary to be overly precise in this step.

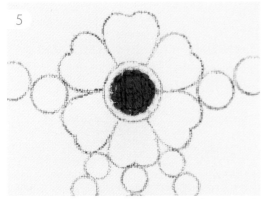

5

Embroider vertical satin stitches above the first layer of padding, filling the circle completely. Make sure to bring the needle in and out close to the backstitch outline.

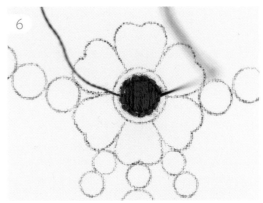

6

Switch to a single strand of 190# embroidery thread and embroider the outermost layer with satin stitch. Start from the center of the circle and ensure that both the entry and exit points of the needle are on the drawn outline.

7

Start by embroidering the satin stitch from the center and work toward one side of the upper half. Once one side is completed, proceed to embroider the other side of the lower half with satin stitch. When pulling the thread, control the tension carefully to create a slightly raised and rounded arc on the embroidered surface.

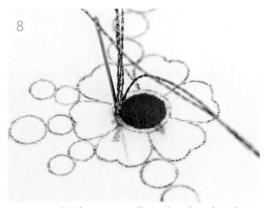

8

Use 3 strands of E301# metallic embroidery threads as the central line for the couching stitch. Then, take another strand of the same thread as the fixing thread and begin couching along the outside of the red circle's center.

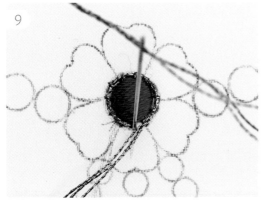

9

After completing one circle of couching stitches, bring the three strands of metallic embroidery threads back to the starting point and secure them by inserting the needle into the fabric to finish the stitching.

10

The image depicts the effect after handling the thread ends.

11

Use double-strand 713# embroidery threads to stitch the outline of the petal with backstitch. However, only stitch the outline of the upper half of the petal at this point. The next step of padded satin stitch should also only pad the upper half of the petal, rather than padding the entire petal uniformly. This technique will create the effect that the flower petals raised on the outside and with concave on the inside.

12

Continue using double-strand 713# embroidery threads to pad the first layer of the flower petal using satin stitch. Embroider vertically, allowing slight gaps between the stitches of the first layer. Again, only embroider the upper half of the petal, leaving space between the outline stitches for the second layer of padding.

13

Embroider the second layer using horizontal satin stitch, covering the first layer of stitches completely. Continue embroidering until reaching about two-thirds of the petal's length. For the second layer of padding, ensure that there are no gaps between the stitches and maintain a smooth, even appearance throughout the embroidery.

14

Use single-strand 713# embroidery thread to embroider the outermost layer of the flower petal. Start from the center of the pattern, and for the first stitch, bring the needle out from the outline of the petal. For the second stitch, insert the needle from the edge of the lower layer of padding, creating a long stitch.

15

For the third and fourth stitches, create a shorter stitch approximately two-thirds the length of the first and second stitches. Make sure to insert the needle perpendicularly to avoid disrupting the texture of the lower padded satin stitch.

16

Finish the right half of the flower petal using a stitching pattern of alternating long and short stitches.

Continue embroidering to complete the other half of the flower petal on the left side.

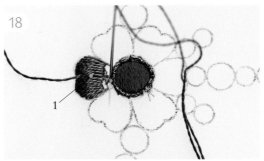

Use single-strand 714# embroidery thread to continue embroidering the lower half of the flower petal using the long and short stitch method. For the first stitch, bring the needle out from the short stitch's tail at the center of the petal (position 1). For the second stitch, insert the needle right next to the edge of the metallic thread that forms the center of the petal. (The image is rotated to show the stitches clearly.)

For the third stitch, bring the needle out from the tail of the adjacent long stitch, creating a height difference between the third and first stitches. It is essential to be flexible with the exit and entry points of the stitches in this batch. Bringing the needle out precisely between the two previous stitches or from the line of the previous stitch is not a strict requirement. Instead, you can adjust the placement of the stitches according to the desired density and spacing in the embroidery. (The image is rotated to show the stitches clearly.)

Complete the lower half of this flower petal using the long and short stitch technique.

Using the same method, embroider the remaining five petals in a similar manner.

Use single-strand metallic embroidery thread in E699# as the center line for the couching stitch. Then, take a single-strand 257# embroidery thread as the fixing thread and couch along the outline of the circular shape.

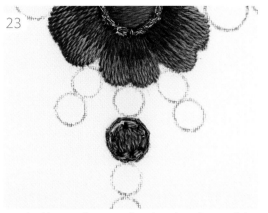

23

24

Use double-strand 257# embroidery threads to pad the interior of the circular shape. Leave a distance of about 0.5 mm between the backstitch outline and the metallic couching stitch. Embroider the first layer of horizontal satin stitches followed by a second layer of vertical satin stitches to fill the area inside the backstitch outline.

Embroider the surface of the circular shape using single-strand 257# embroidery thread with horizontal satin stitch.

25

26

The image depicts the effect after completion.

Using the same method, embroider the other three large green circles.

27

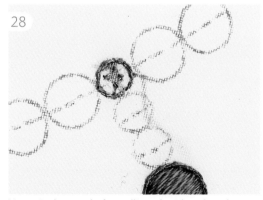

28

Next, embroider the bead pattern in a continuous string. Before embroidering, you can use a heat erasable pen to draw auxiliary lines, as shown in the picture, in the middle of each circle. The direction represented by these auxiliary lines will be used as a reference for embroidering the outermost layer satin stitches with a raised effect.

Use a single strand of metallic embroidery thread E301# as the centerline and a single strand of 713# embroidery thread as the fixing thread. Embroider the circular outline in the picture using the couching stitch. Start and finish all stitches at the center position of the circle, replacing the first layer of padding stitches.

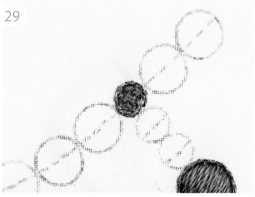

29

Due to the small size of this circle, the padded part on the inside will continue to be embroidered using a single strand of 713# embroidery thread. First, use the backstitch to outline the circular shape, and then for the satin stitch part, only embroider one layer vertically, perpendicular to the direction of the auxiliary line.

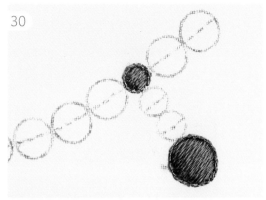

30

Continue using a single strand of 713# embroidery thread to embroider the surface with satin stitch. The direction of the stitches should be the same as the direction of the auxiliary line.

31

Using the same method, embroider the other side's small brown circle.

32

Use a single strand of metallic embroidery thread E3747# as the centerline for the couching stitch. Use a single strand of 430# embroidery thread as the fixing thread. Embroider the circular outline in the picture using the couching stitch. Start and finish all stitches at the center position of the circle, replacing the first layer of padding stitches.

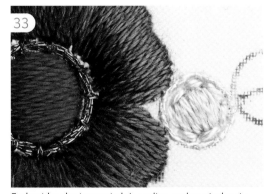

33

Embroider the inner circle's outline and vertical satin stitches using a double-strand of 430# embroidery threads.

34

Embroider the surface with satin stitch using a single-strand of 430# embroidery thread. The direction of the stitches should be the same as the direction of the auxiliary line.

35

Using the same method, embroider all the large light gray circles.

36

Continue embroidering the small light gray circles. Use a single strand of metallic embroidery thread E3747# as the centerline for the couching stitch. Use a single strand of 430# embroidery thread as the fixing thread. Embroider the circular outline in the picture using the couching stitch method. All starting and ending stitches should be done at the center position of each circle, replacing the first layer of padding stitches. After that, use a single strand of 430# embroidery thread to embroider the outline with backstitch and vertical satin stitch.

37

Embroider the surface with satin stitch using a single-strand of 430# embroidery thread. The direction of the stitches should be the same as the direction of the auxiliary lines.

38

Using the same method, embroider all the small light gray circles.

39

Repeat steps 28 to 30 for the remaining four brown circles. Once you have finished embroidering all the circles, your work is complete.

CHAPTER FOUR
Projects

This chapter explains six large embroidery projects, each of which incorporates various embroidery techniques from Chapter Three. When studying the projects in this chapter, if you are not familiar with certain techniques, you can refer to the corresponding techniques and their detailed explanations in Chapter Three. The projects in this chapter, aside from *Ocean Waves* in goldwork embroidery, are arranged from easy to difficult, serving as a reference for the reader's learning progression.

Finally, it should be noted that embroidery can be viewed as painting with needles and threads instead of brushes and ink. While there are many techniques, rules, and guidelines that have been summarized by previous practitioners and passed down through generations, the most exceptional embroidery artists have repeatedly emphasized that there are no fixed rules. This means that embroidery techniques are not rigid and unchanging. To create outstanding pieces, one must carefully observe the object being embroidered, thoroughly understand its structure and colors, and apply embroidery techniques flexibly as needed. This is the key to producing exceptional embroidery works.

The actual sized paper patterns of the six projects can be found in the gatefold at the end of the book. The brands of embroidery threads used for the projects are listed in the Materials part and only color numbers are written in the text of the step instructions. In the Color Thread Diagram, the brand name of DMC or ANCHOR will be marked for easy reference.

Fig. 65 The projects of *Auspicious Clouds* (see page 55), *Water Waves* (see page 69), and *Taihu Stone* (see page 131).

1. Ocean Waves

During China's Song dynasty, the wave pattern became popular. The prominent Southern Song artist Ma Yuan (1140–1225) created the work *Water Album*, consisting of twelve paintings vividly depicting various water scenarios such as the misty expanse of lakes, the surging and rushing of river waves, and the roaring and raging of the boundless sea. The wave pattern also carries the metaphor of carrying virtues and accommodating all things, symbolizing the virtue of benevolence and the ability to embrace diversity. It was often used as embroidery on ancient official robes, serving as a symbol of social status.

This piece is done entirely using the goldwork embroidery technique. During the embroidery process, each individual section is embroidered separately according to the pattern. The main challenge of the work lies in handling various intricate details, such as sharp angles, turns, choosing between single and double strands, and determining the stitching path. It is important to note that the execution of goldwork embroidery is not fixed, and a single design might include several different approaches to stitching paths.

Materials

Base fabric: antique-style organza.

Embroidery threads: gold embroidery thread 5# gold color; **OLYMPUS** No. 25 embroidery thread 512# (single strand).

Color Thread Diagram

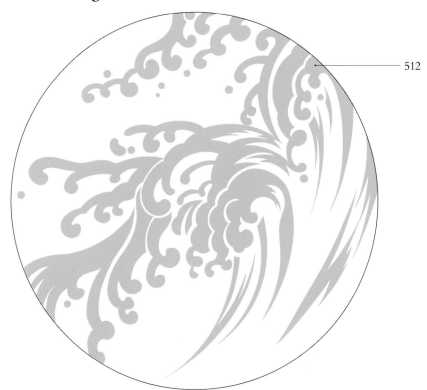

512

Steps

When embroidering sharp angles, you should stitch each strand of the double-strand threads separately to ensure that the sharp angles remain sharp and do not lose their shape, but stay firmly in place.

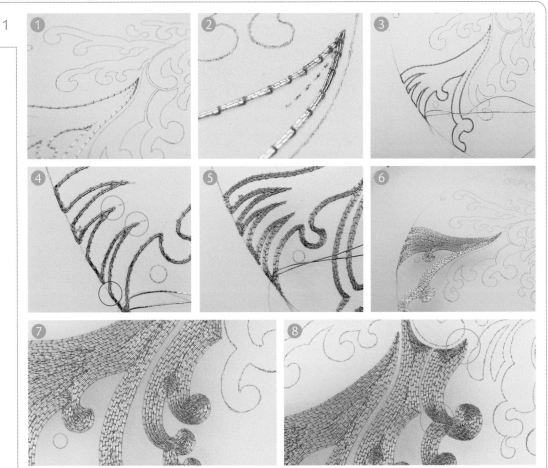

Embroidery Details for Step 1: Figures 1–2 depict the precise corner embroidery effect of the outer contour line. When embroidering sharp angles, start by securing the sharp corner of the outer line. Once the bending shape of the outer line is properly fixed, proceed to embroider the bending shape of the inner line (refer to details in figures 1 and 2). For angles greater than 90 degrees, the two strands of threads are essentially stitched side by side (refer to figure 3 and the details marked with the red circle in figure 4). For angles smaller than 90 degrees, a slight gap between the sharp corner of the inner thread and the sharp corner of the outer thread is necessary to achieve a better bend (refer to the details marked with green circles in figure 4). Figures 5 and 6 illustrate the method used to maintain sharp corners while keeping the internal lines smooth. Figures 7 and 8 demonstrate a method where the internal corners are not kept sharp. When stitching the two threads separately, there is minimal gap, and the curvature of the corner becomes progressively smoother as layers of gold embroidery are added inward (as indicated by the green circle annotations). This approach is suitable for beginners and is a relatively straightforward method for handling corners.

For patterns with significant variations in width and narrowness, it is important to handle the direction of the gold threads flexibly. You should determine when to break the threads and when to transition from double strands to single strands for coiling.

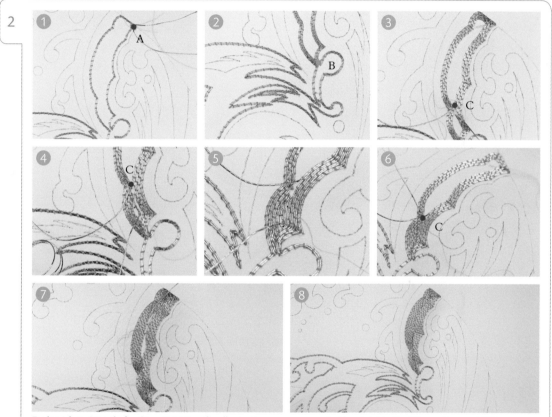

Embroidery Details for Step 2: Using the illustration as an example, the right half of the pattern exhibits noticeable changes in width, particularly at the junction of the two segments, which is especially narrow. Starting from point A in figure 1, begin embroidering. After completing the outer contour line, return to the starting point and continue with the second layer. As you embroider toward the junction point B in figure 2, there is only enough space for the double strands to pass through once. At this point, as shown in figure 2, you can opt to create a folded corner with the double strands. Continue embroidering toward the right edge, forming a closed shape for this segment before proceeding with the goldwork embroidery. When stitching the third layer to point C, there is only enough space for 2 strands of threads to pass through. To minimize thread breaks, you can, as shown in figure 3, let one strand on the left side remain idle and continue stitching downward with the single strand on the right side. To allow this strand to exit from point C, it is necessary to design the path of the inner line below point C. Refer to figure 4: After completing a small circle of stitches with this strand, when starting the second circle of stitches, maintain a one-thread space from the adjacent stitched thread, as indicated by the red mark showing distance. Follow the path indicated by the black line in figure 5, couching the thread as shown in figure 6 toward point C and continue double-strand thread stitching along with the idle thread to fill the shape. As shown in figure 7, when reaching the central position, if there isn't sufficient room for double-strand couching, you can separate a single strand to stitch and couch for the finishing.

When dealing with elongated patterns, it is advisable to flexibly use both single and double strands of threads. In areas where it is not suitable to fold the thread back, consider breaking the thread as a solution.

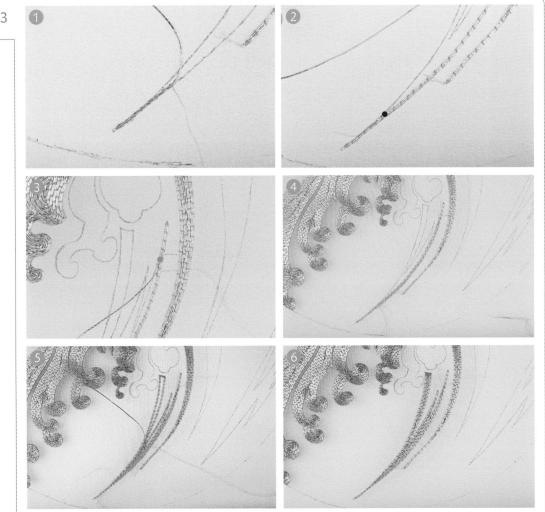

Embroidery Details for Step 3: As shown in figure 1, to maintain a sharp and slender shape when starting, you can use a single strand of gold thread to stitch a section. Once you reach a point where there is enough width for double strands of threads, add the second strand and continue stitching, as indicated by the red dot in figure 2. As you embroider toward the top, you can fold back the outer line as shown in figure 3, but the inner line can be broken (as indicated by the green dot in figure 3). As shown in figure 4, when embroidering the outer line to the lower tail end, due to the slender shape of the pattern, folding back the thread might disrupt the smooth outline. At this point, you can break the thread and start anew, as shown in figure 5, to continue embroidering the outer contour line. Finally, use a single strand of thread to fill in the remaining gaps.

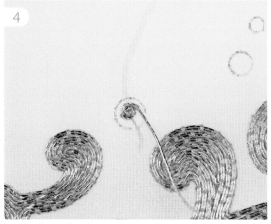
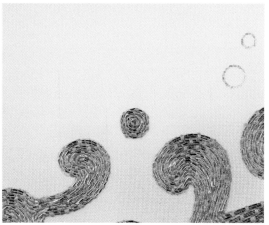

For small circular shapes, the stitching method involves starting from the center and coiling the single thread outward until completing the entire circle. This approach offers the advantage of tightly coiled lines and prevents the occurrence of larger gaps inside when coiling from the outside inward.

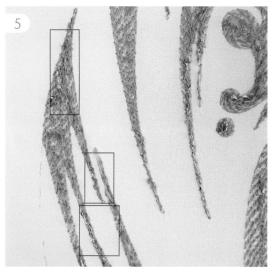

The illustration depicts two methods for handling the gold thread on the back side. If the cut end of the gold thread is within the shape, you can trim it to 3–5 mm. It just needs to be out of sight from the front (as indicated by the green circles). For gold threads at the outer edge and top of the shape, use embroidery thread to simply secure them on the back side of the embroidery, within the shape, and then trim them short (see red squares).

The images depict the completed work.

2. Camellia

The camellia is native to China. It has a graceful plant posture, lush, glossy leaves, and vibrant, colorful flowers. It blooms during the winter and spring, displaying a proud spirit similar to that of the plum blossom. It is one of the ten most popular flowers in China.

Materials

Base fabric: antique-style organza.

Embroidery threads: **OLYMPUS** No. 25 embroidery threads 801#, 512#, 514#, 701#, 655#, 218#, 274#, 265# and 7025# (single strand).

Color Thread Diagram

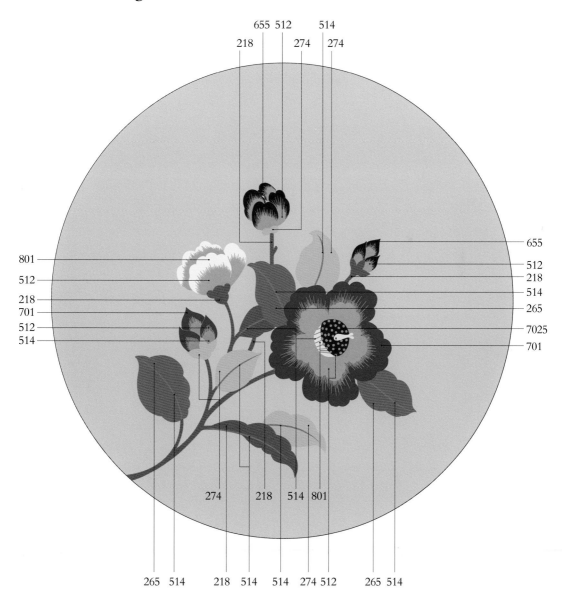

Steps

Start by embroidering the bottom layer of the design, including some branches and leaves. Use the diagonal satin stitch for the branches. For the leaves, employ the long and short shaded satin stitch, paying special attention to the direction of the stitch alignment.

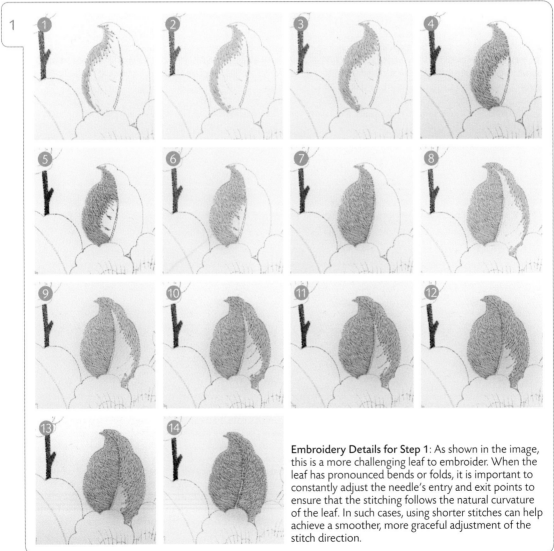

Embroidery Details for Step 1: As shown in the image, this is a more challenging leaf to embroider. When the leaf has pronounced bends or folds, it is important to constantly adjust the needle's entry and exit points to ensure that the stitching follows the natural curvature of the leaf. In such cases, using shorter stitches can help achieve a smoother, more graceful adjustment of the stitch direction.

2

When embroidering the edge of the front leaf, make sure to cover the edge of the back leaf to prevent any gaps and ensure a smooth, seamless edge.

3

Use the long and short shaded satin stitch to embroider the flower receptacles and flower buds. When embroidering, ensure that the stitch direction of the two colors of threads on a single petal remains consistent. Take note that the yellow portion on the purple flower bud should be embroidered using 512#. On the red flower bud, the yellow portion should be embroidered using both 512# and 514#.

3

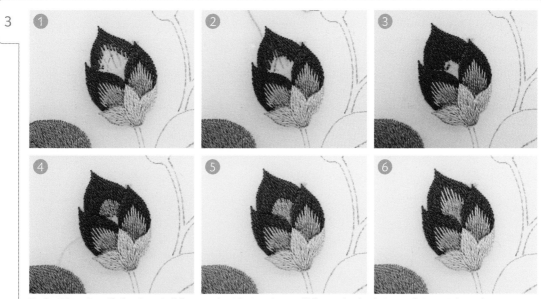

Embroidery Details for Step 3: When embroidering the small flower buds, their small size might make it challenge to embroider one layer of petals over the other. In this case, you can start by embroidering the flower receptacle, then move on to the small petals, working upwards one layer at a time. Ensure that there are no gaps between the petals and try to keep them as close together as possible. When embroidering a single small petal, start from the tip and work inward. The petal is divided into upper and lower sections by an auxiliary line. Begin by using red embroidery thread to stitch the upper half of the petal. Employ the long and short shaded satin stitch for this, but when reaching the final layer, make sure that the needle goes in along the auxiliary line to create an outline. Use yellow thread to embroider the lower half. Start by using 514# to stitch along the edge of the red thread, and then continue using the long and short shaded satin stitch to fill the remaining area. From there, create a beautiful thread-like vein by intermittently stitching a few long stitches using 512# along the boundary between the red and yellow sections.

4

Use the slanted stem stitch to embroider the leaf veins. Generally, start from the tip and work toward the base of the vein, paying attention to varying the stitch length to depict the changing thickness of the veins.

5

When embroidering the large camellia flower, begin by embroidering the petal sections. The petals are generally completed using two sets of colors. The left image consists of yellow and red, while the right image combines yellow and white. Use the long and short shaded satin stitch for embroidery.

5

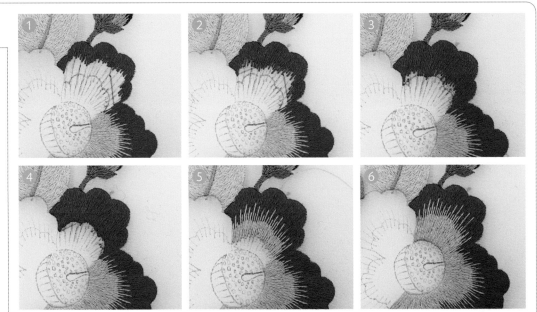

Embroidery Details for Step 5: As depicted in the image, the large petal is divided into upper and lower sections by an auxiliary line. The upper half is embroidered in the same method as the flower bud, following the previously mentioned technique. Use yellow thread to embroider the lower half. When embroidering the first batch, alternate between long and short stitches. For the short stitches, bring the needle out along the outline of the red section, and for the long stitches, bring it out from deeper within the red part. You can vary the lengths of the long stitches to create a detailed, intricate texture resembling the veins of the petal. For the remaining area, continue filling the petal using the long and short shaded satin stitch. If you find that some of the yellow long stitches aren't long enough, you can add another stitch to make them longer and slightly curved for a more graceful appearance. Note that when the petal meets the leaf, you should first complete the lower layer of the leaf. Embroider the petal's thread over the edge of the leaf's embroidery to ensure a smooth transition.

The central part of the flower is embroidered using the long and short shaded satin stitch and knot stitch.

The finished result is shown in the image.

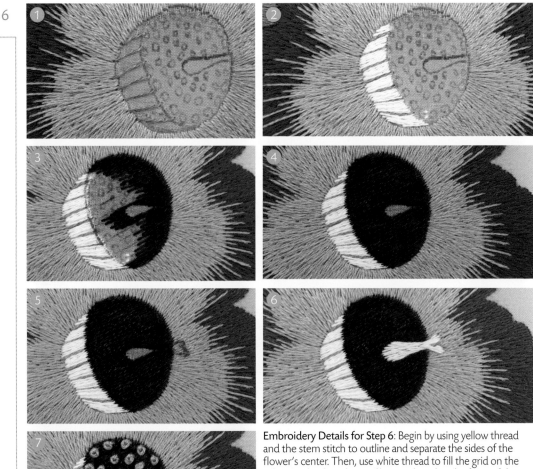

Embroidery Details for Step 6: Begin by using yellow thread and the stem stitch to outline and separate the sides of the flower's center. Then, use white thread to fill the grid on the sides. Apply a base layer of brown thread to the front of the flower's stamens. Use the long and short shaded satin stitch for the base of sides and front. Embroider the central white pistil using the long and short stitch. Before embroidering, you can use a heat erasable pen to draw the complete shape for guidance (see figure 5). Finally, use double-strand yellow embroidery threads to create double-loop knots from the outer edge toward the center, embellishing the entire flower's core.

3. Butterfly in Love with Flowers

In this artwork, the butterfly is more intricate both in terms of technique and thread colors compared to the *Butterfly* in the technique introduction of long and short shaded satin stitch (see page 117). The combination of butterflies and flowers is a classic motif in Chinese embroidery, symbolizing beauty and happiness.

Materials

Base fabric: transparent organza.

Embroidery threads: **OLYMPUS** No. 25 embroidery threads 2041#, 440#, 214#, 101#, 143#, 331#, 736#, 415#, 744#, 205#, 801#, 2012#, 414#, 752#, 5205#; **DMC** No. 25 embroidery threads 349#, 3021#, 437# (single strand).

Color Thread Diagram

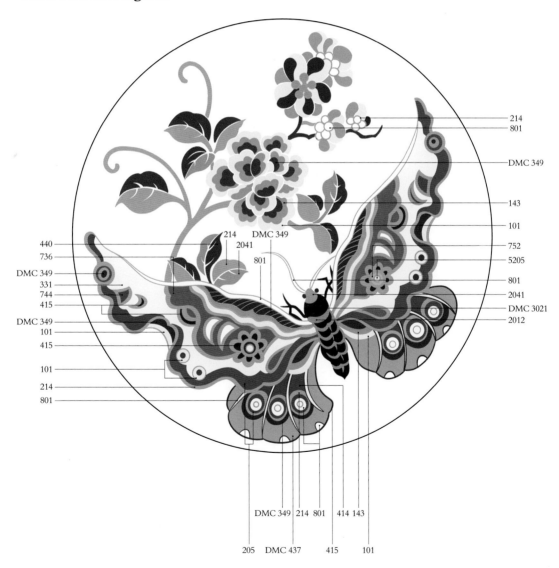

Steps

Begin by embroidering the leaves using the long and short shaded satin stitch, leaving the leaf veins blank. Then, use the satin stitch to embroider the vines and branches.

Use the satin stitch, long and short shaded satin stitch, and stem stitch techniques to embroider the flowers and branches in the upper part.

Embroidery Details for Step 1: As shown in the image, this is a more challenging leaf with a very full curvature. The direction of the first batch of stitches is particularly important, so be careful to adjust the stitch direction accordingly. When embroidering each subsequent batch, it is important to consider how to align the stitch direction to match the curvature of the design. In such cases, using shorter stitch lengths can make adjusting the stitch direction smoother and more gentle.

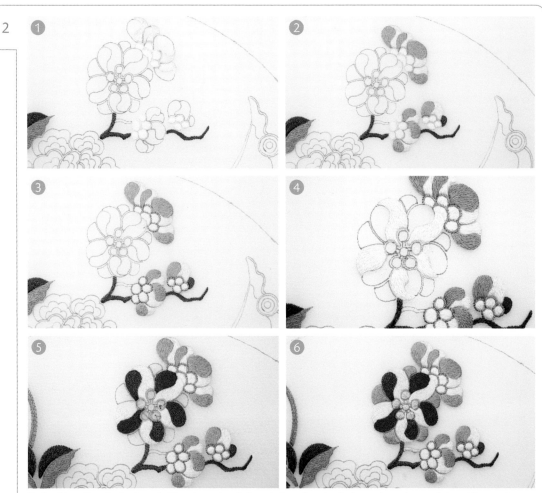

Embroidery Details for Step 2: Use the satin stitch technique for the dark gray branches and the white sepals, as well as the blue parts of the stamen. Each petal is divided into two shades: light and dark. Embroider the light pink portion first, followed by the dark pink part. Use the long and short shaded satin stitch technique with slightly shorter stitches, paying attention to the changes in curvature. There should be no gaps between the dark and light shades on a single petal, but leave some space (or waterway) between the individual petals and between petals and sepals. Embroider a green border around the outer edge of the white sepals using the stem stitch technique.

For the larger flower, you can use the basic encroaching satin stitch technique, where each color is embroidered using the satin stitch with one layer overlapping another. Alternatively, as shown in the illustration, you can use the long and short shaded satin stitch technique instead of the satin stitch for each color. This allows for more freedom and richness in the transitions.

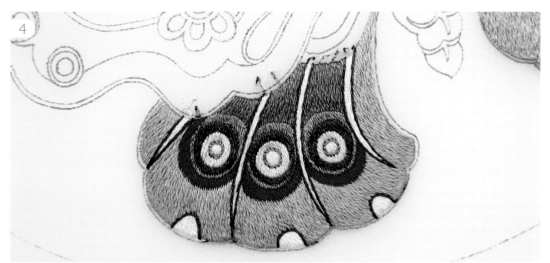

When embroidering the butterfly, start by embroidering the small wings. Use the long and short shaded satin stitch technique for large areas of filling and the satin stitch technique for smaller areas. Use the stem stitch technique for the dark gray outlines. Begin by embroidering the earthy yellow and gray sections. Then, work from the outer layer toward the center to embroider the concentric circular patterns. Leave a gap between the innermost white circle and the second-to-last light blue circle, and use the stem stitch technique with green thread to fill the gap.

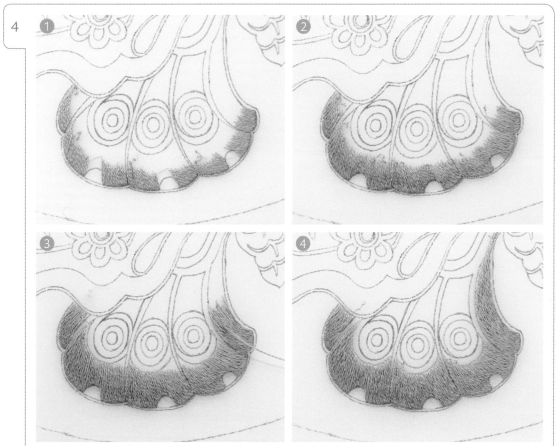

Embroidery Details for Step 4: The earthy yellow section is relatively large and has a gentle curvature. You can follow the details shown in the above four images and use the long and short shaded satin stitch technique in layers to create a soft, smooth curvature.

Use the slanted stem stitch technique to embroider the outline of the small wings. Once completed, use the same method as embroidering the larger flower to embroider the remaining white, pink, and red sections of the small wings.

As shown in the illustration, start by embroidering the large sections of the large wings. Similarly, use the long and short shaded satin stitch technique to embroider from the outer edge toward the center in sequence.

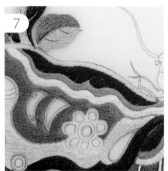

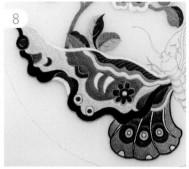

When embroidering the red section of the large wings, leave space for the veins. After completing the red section, use the stem stitch technique with green thread to embroider the veins.

Continue filling in the remaining areas of the large wings. Use the long and short shaded satin stitch technique for larger areas and the satin stitch technique for smaller areas. The stitch direction can be referenced from the above image.

Finally, embroider the green outlines along the edges and inside of the large wings. Use the satin stitch technique for thicker sections and the slanted stem stitch technique for finer lines along the upper edge of the wings.

Use the same method to embroider the wings on the opposite side. Finally, embroider the body of the butterfly. For the eyes, feet, and antennae, use the satin stitch technique for the interior filling. Use the stem stitch technique for the outline of the antennae. Embroider the body part from the tail to the head. Use the long and short shaded satin stitch technique for the brown and light blue sections and the satin stitch technique for the green section.

4. Chinese Flowering Crabapple

The Chinese flowering crabapple, often referred to as *haitanghua*, is known for its graceful, elegant appearance, earning it the nickname "the fairy among flowers." It is often planted alongside other beautiful flowers like magnolias, peonies, and osmanthus, symbolizing prosperity and wealth, often represented as *yutang fugui* in Chinese culture. Chinese traditional painting has featured numerous masterpieces centered around the theme of the Chinese flowering crabapple, making it an excellent subject for embroidery in China, as it offers intricate and captivating details for artists to replicate.

Materials

Base fabric: antique-style organza.

Embroidery threads: **OLYMPUS** No. 25 embroidery threads 100#, 103#, 104#, 105#, 1011#, 1085#, 154#, 155#, 156#, 2011#, 2012#, 2014#, 2015#, 276#, 2835#, 293#, 294#, 769#, 783#, 784#, 785#, 786#; **DMC** No. 25 embroidery threads 3031#, 3345#, 3346#, 367#, 420#, 469#, 580#, 733#, 830#, 937#, 987#, 727#, 963#, 3831#, 3777#, 3857# (single strand).

Color Thread Diagram

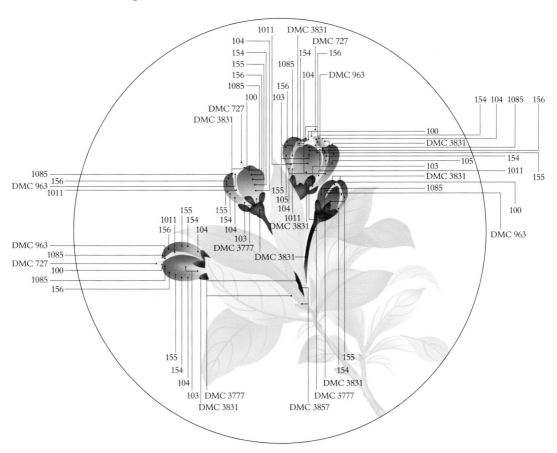

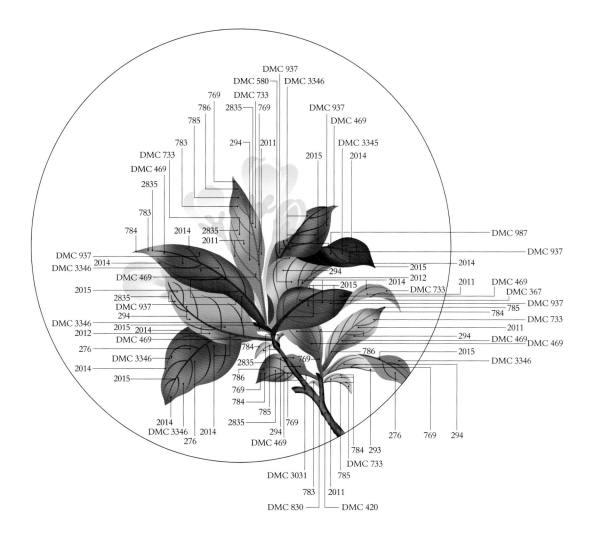

Steps

Start by embroidering the three crabapple flower buds located at the bottom, hidden behind the leaves. When embroidering, follow the same sequence of stitching the petals from back to front. If the petals have a lighter colored inner exposed portion, embroider the inner part first and then the outer part. While embroidering, use long and short shaded satin stitch for the petals, long and short stitches for the receptacle, and satin stitches for the stamen. Please note that the fourth flower bud on the far right should be embroidered after completing the leaves.

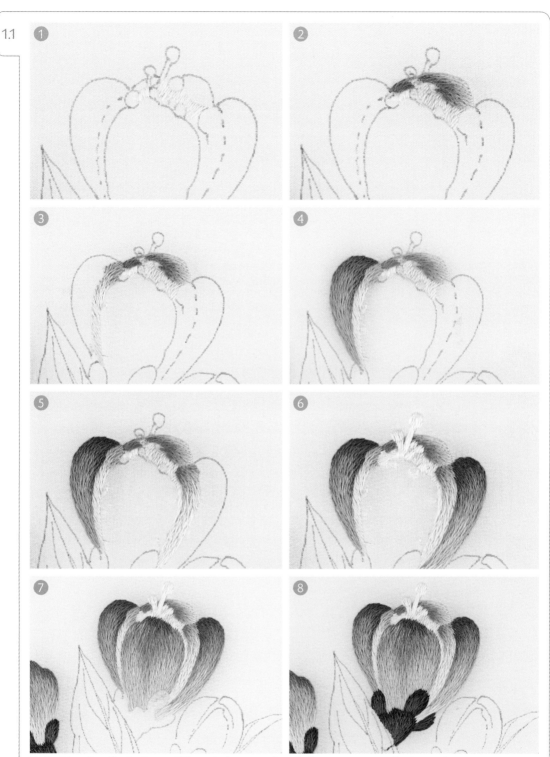

Embroidery Detail 1 for Step 1: Taking the largest crabapple flower as an example, the stitching sequence is as follows. First, embroider the light pink at the center of the flower. Then, embroider the small exposed part of the petal at the back. Following the order in the diagram, for each petal, start by embroidering the lighter inner exposed part. Next, embroider the darker outer part of the petal. Continue this sequence for each petal to complete the entire flower bud. Finally, embroider the receptacle.

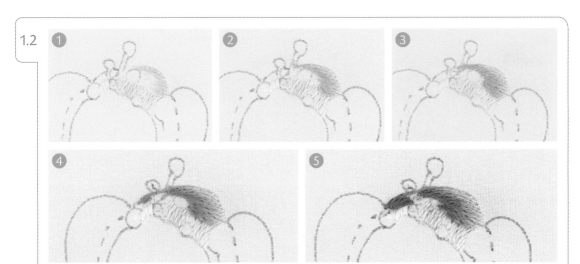

Embroidery Detail 2 for Step 1: The embroidered details of the petals are illustrated with two petals. The five images above show the embroidery method for the small petals at the back. You can start from the outer contour edge and gradually work from light to dark, using single-strand threads in the following sequence: 103#, 104#, 154#, 155# and 156#. Embroider these petals using long and short shaded satin stitch.

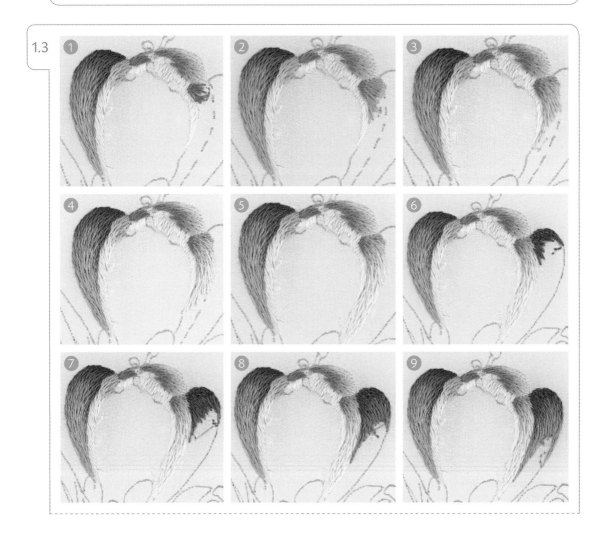

Embroidery Detail 3 for Step 1: The twelve images on facing page and above illustrate the embroidery method for the right-side petal. First, use single-strand threads in the following sequence: 156#, 155#, 154#, 103# and 1011#. Start from the top and work your way down using long and short shaded satin stitch to complete the lighter side of the petal. Then, use single-strand threads in the following sequence: DMC 3831#, OLYMPUS 1085#, 156#, 155#, 105#, 104# and 103#. Start from the top and work your way down using long and short shaded satin stitch to complete the darker side of the petal. The top of the crabapple flower bud curls toward the center, so when embroidering in the area near the top of the petal, use shorter stitches and pay special attention to the stitch direction for smooth transitions.

1.4

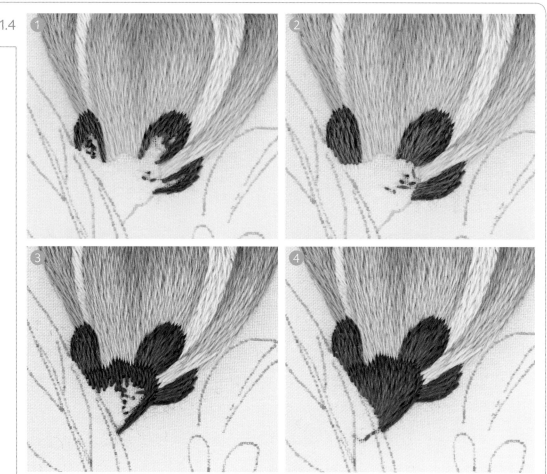

Embroidery Detail 4 for Step 1: The four images above illustrate the embroidery method for the receptacle. Use single-strand threads 3777# and 3831# to embroider with long and short stitch, the darker thread for the outer edges and the lighter thread for filling the interior.

2

The colors of the leaves can be primarily divided into three categories, deep green, lighter shades of green, the most complex part is the leaf tips, which have a yellow-brown coloration. When embroidering, follow the color numbers marked on the diagram and embroider using long and short shaded satin stitch from the leaf tip to the root. However, it is important to note that each batch of colors doesn't strictly transition from the outer edge of the leaf to the inside. When embroidering, carefully observe the range of color changes while also considering the stitch direction to make the leaves appear dynamic and lifelike.

2.1

Embroidery Detail 1 for Step 2:
When embroidering the leaves, it is advisable to start from the bottommost leaves, following the embroidery sequence shown in the images above.

2.2

① ② ③

④ ⑤ ⑥

⑦ ⑧ ⑨

⑩

Embroidery Detail 2 for Step 2: When embroidering the leaves, start from the tip, following the steps shown in the diagrams. Use single-strand threads in the following sequence: OLYMPUS 769#, 786#, 785#, 783#, 2835#, DMC 733#, OLYMPUS 2011#, 294# and DMC 469#. Stitch from the top down using long and short shaded satin stitch to cover the entire leaf. After completing the leaf surface, use 769# single-strand thread to embroider the leaf veins using the slanted stem stitch technique. When embroidering the leaf veins, start by embroidering the finer veins on both sides before working on the central main vein. Similarly, embroider from the tip of the vein toward the root when working on the veins.

3

4

Finally, embroider the branches. Since the branches are relatively thin, you can use long and short stitch. Start by outlining with 3031#, and then fill the interior with single-strand threads in 830# and 420#. To enhance the wood texture of the branches, you can blend 830# and 420# threads when embroidering the interior of the branches.

The image depicts the finished result.

5. The Lotus

The lotus has long been praised because it "emerges from the mud without being stained," and it is a common subject in the works of painters. This embroidery piece imitates the summer lotus in Song dynasty paintings, portraying the lotus in intricate detail with swaying aquatic plants, as if a breeze is blowing by.

Materials

Base fabric: antique-style organza.

Embroidery threads: **OLYMPUS** No. 25 embroidery threads 212#, 288#, 284#, 2835#, 214#, 207#, 2070#, 202#, 203#, 2071#, 2072#, 244#, 2445#, 245#, 253#, 263#, 1013#, 1032#, 1031#, 1900#, 1120#, 1014#, 161#, 1898#, 1011#, 103#, 102#, 1033#; **DMC** No. 25 embroidery threads 732#, 469#, 163#, 730#, 561# (single strand).

Color Thread Diagram

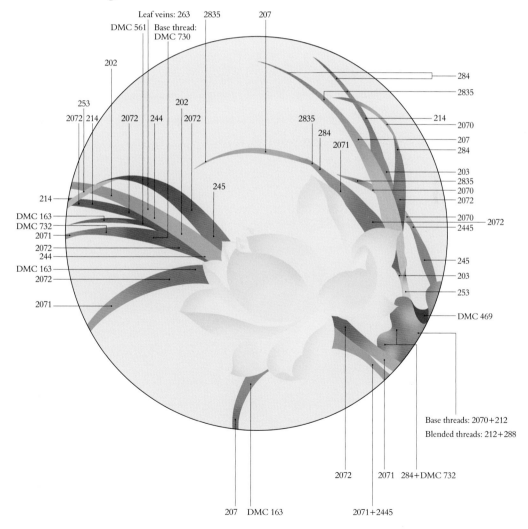

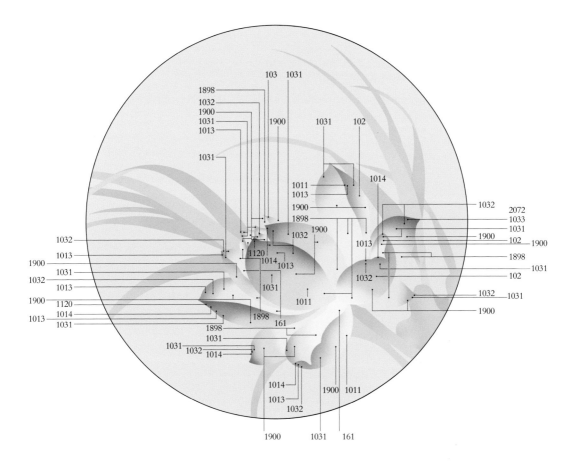

Steps

1

For the complete embroidery, you can generally follow the sequence of first embroidering the lower layer's pattern and then embroidering the overlaying pattern on top of it. First, embroider the delicate leaves of water plants. While embroidering, work from the tip of the leaf toward the base, using a combination of long and short shaded satin stitch and blended (long and short) stitch. The stitching arrangement can be relatively flexible.

1

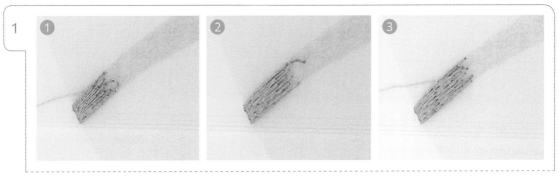

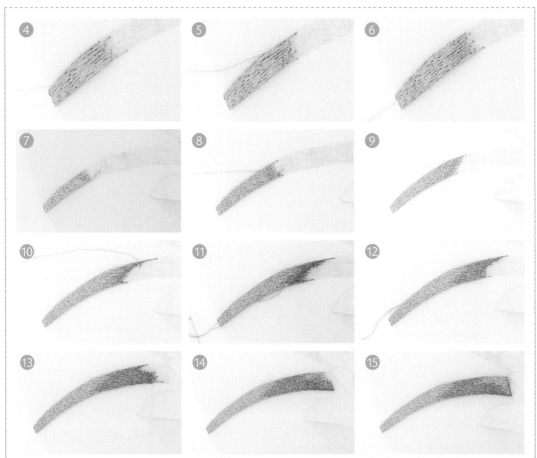

Embroidery Details for Step 1: Taking the leaf shown in the image as an example, first embroider the initial section using a single strand of OLYMPUS 2071# embroidery thread. Use long and short shaded satin stitch, progressing batch by batch, until you reach the position indicated in figure 9. Next, embroider the areas indicated in figures 10 to 12 using a single strand of 2071# embroidery thread. Finally, complete the remaining sections of the leaf using a single strand of DMC 163# embroidery thread. When embroidering, pay close attention to the variation in the length of your stitches, especially when using the long and short shaded satin stitch technique. Failure to achieve this variation might result in a rigid, monotonous appearance in the shading.

2

Continue embroidering the water plant leaves on the right side. These leaves have a yellow-green tip, creating a more pronounced color contrast. Pay attention to the variation in your stitching when transitioning between colors. Strive for natural transitions at the junctions between different colors. In areas with many turns and narrow spaces, you can combine the use of blended stitch and long and short shaded satin stitch. For instance, at the tip of the leaf, you can employ the blended stitch technique.

2

①

②

③

④

⑤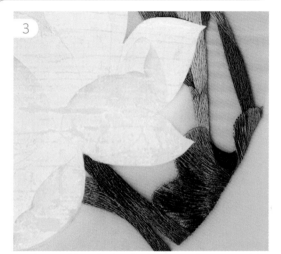

3

Embroidery Details for Step 2: For the leaf tip in figure 1, use a single strand of 2835# embroidery thread and employ blended stitch to achieve a delicate, natural look. At the area marked in figure 2, use a single strand of 207# embroidery thread and interweave it with the previous color for stitching. Continue until completing the color section as shown in figure 3. In figure 4, use a single strand of 2835# embroidery thread to transition from the 207# thread. Then, blend in a single strand of 284# embroidery thread to enhance the leaf's golden-yellow color. In figure 5, start by using a single strand of 2071# embroidery thread to embroider the left side of the leaf. Then, transition toward the lower right corner by switching to 2072# embroidery thread to allow the leaf to change from light green to a deeper shade of green.

For the small lotus leaf in the bottom right corner of the image, start by using long and short shaded satin stitch to establish the basic color transition. Once the base color is complete, use blended stitch on the surface to add some intermingling and collision of colors.

4

The embroidery of the lotus follows the sequence of first embroidering the lowest layer of petals and then proceeding to the upper layers, using long and short shaded satin stitch for all the petals. Embroidering lotus petals can be quite challenging, mainly due to their plump, rounded shape, which requires careful consideration of the stitch direction. At the same time, the color transitions should appear natural. The pink portions should not be too dominant, and you should leave enough space for the light pink and white areas so that the coloration of the lotus petals won't appear clumsy and will maintain a graceful appearance.

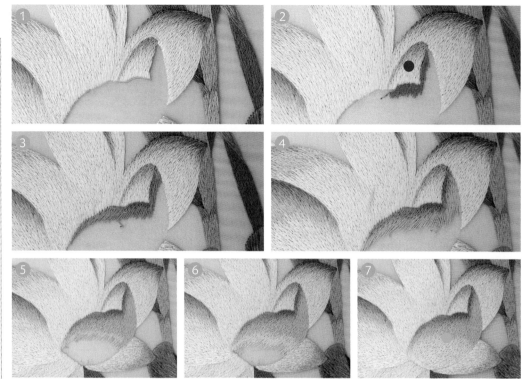

Embroidery Details for Step 4: Lotus petals come in two different states, fully open and partially folded. When dealing with folded petals, you should first embroider the inner side of the petal (as marked by the red dot in figure 2) and then embroider the outer side (as marked by the green dot in figure 7). As shown in figure 1, this petal is initially embroidered with a small exposed portion of its inner side. While embroidering, it is important to control the precise contour lines. On the darker side, the stitching should cover the inner contour line of the underlying petal (as indicated by the green line). On the lighter side, the stitching should extend over the contour line of the upcoming outer petal (as indicated by the blue line). Figures 2 through 7 depict the embroidery of the outer petal. In figure 2, use a single strand of 1014# embroidery thread. Figure 3 is a bit unique. It mainly requires a single strand of 1013# embroidery thread. Add 1032# embroidery thread to enhance the delicate color variation. Figures 4 through 7 are then embroidered sequentially using single strands of embroidery threads 1031#, 102#, 1900# and 1898# in turn.

The image depicts the finished result.

6. Kingfisher

This work imitates the Song dynasty painting *Picture of Jade Flowers and Emerald Bird*. The jade flowers and the kingfisher with green feathers symbolize good fortune and auspiciousness, a common theme in ancient Chinese bird-and-flower paintings. In embroidery, birds are a very challenging subject. In this book, the *Kingfisher* is chosen as the final piece, aiming to showcase the integration of various stitching techniques and their flexible application.

Materials

Base fabric: antique-style organza.

Embroidery threads: **OLYMPUS** No. 25 embroidery threads 244#, 245#, 247#, 251#, 255#, 262#, 273#, 274#, 289#, 2014#, 2042#, 352#, 386#, 391#, 416#, 801#, 850#; **DMC** No. 25 embroidery threads 988#, 561#, 518#, 163#, 3799#, 3810#, 924#, 3771#, 945#, 3856#, 402#, 754#, 3809#, 3768# (single strand).

Color Thread Diagram

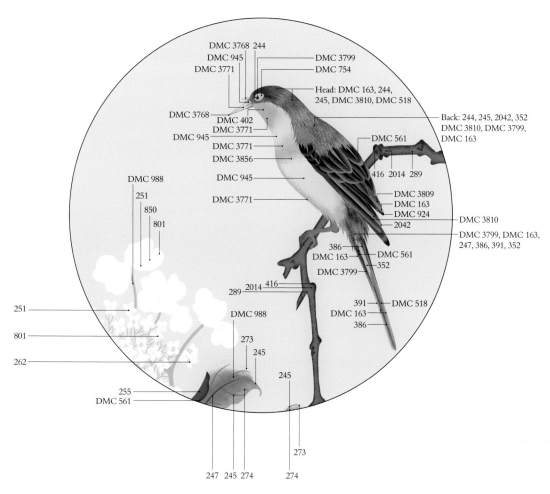

Steps

First, embroider the jade flower and branches in the bottom left corner of the composition. Use blended (long and short) stitch for the larger petals and long and short shaded satin stitch for the leaves. For the smaller flowers' petals and branches, employ satin stitch. Use a single strand of thread to make two rounds of knots for the flower core. Use slanted stem stitch or short stitch as needed for the finer branches and leaves.

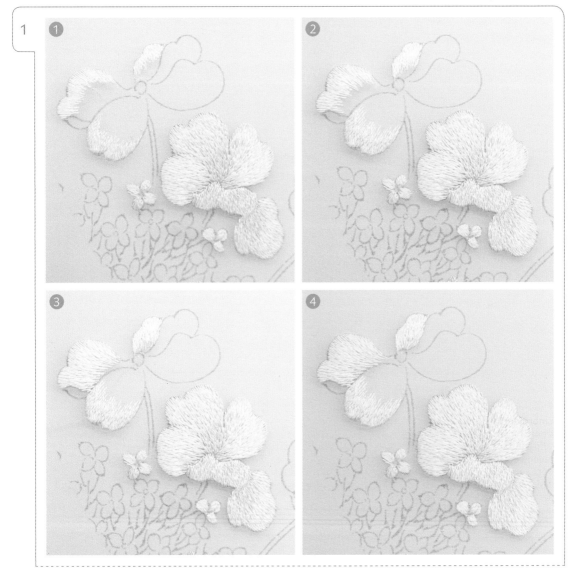

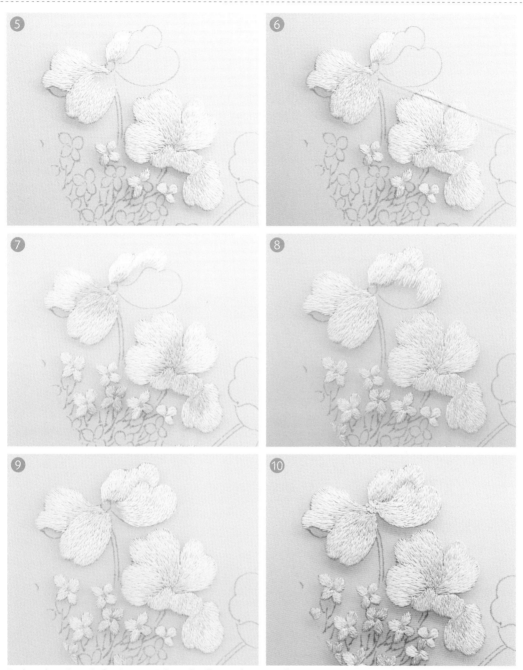

Embroidery Details for Step 1: Taking the flower shown in the images as an example, use single strands of threads in colors 801#, 850#, and 251# in sequence. This will create a transition from white to light green. While embroidering, use long and short stitch, leaving slight gaps between the threads. When inserting the second batch of stitches into the first, emphasize irregularities to give a sense of unevenness, making the petals appear lighter and more delicate. If using long and short shaded satin stitch, with each batch of threads deeply interlaced and closely arranged, the petals will appear thicker. When embroidering, start with the petals that are closer to the back, then embroider the layer in front, stacking them layer by layer without leaving gaps. Finally, use a single strand of thread to create knots for the flower core by wrapping the thread around twice.

If you have extra thread while embroidering, you can use it to embroider small white or light green flowers below.

2

For the narrow branches, using long and short stitch method provides flexibility. Start by embroidering the edges with 416#, then transition to 2014# in the middle, and finally use 289# for the lightest part.

2

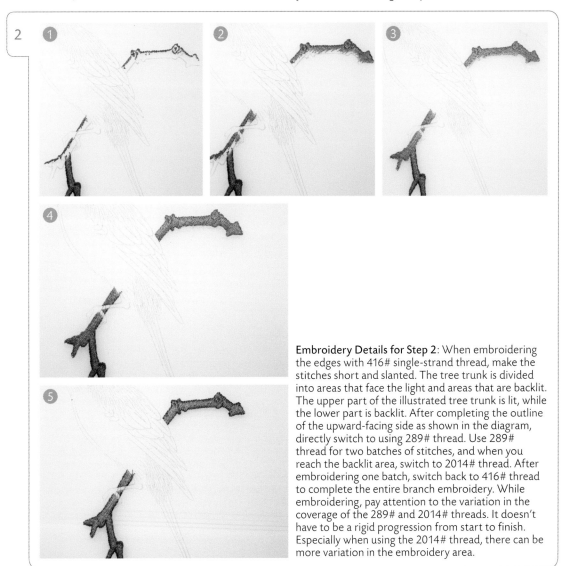

① ② ③ ④ ⑤

Embroidery Details for Step 2: When embroidering the edges with 416# single-strand thread, make the stitches short and slanted. The tree trunk is divided into areas that face the light and areas that are backlit. The upper part of the illustrated tree trunk is lit, while the lower part is backlit. After completing the outline of the upward-facing side as shown in the diagram, directly switch to using 289# thread. Use 289# thread for two batches of stitches, and when you reach the backlit area, switch to 2014# thread. After embroidering one batch, switch back to 416# thread to complete the entire branch embroidery. While embroidering, pay attention to the variation in the coverage of the 289# and 2014# threads. It doesn't have to be a rigid progression from start to finish. Especially when using the 2014# thread, there can be more variation in the embroidery area.

3

The tail feathers and abdomen of the kingfisher are mainly completed using long and short shaded satin stitch and relatively sparse long and short stitch.

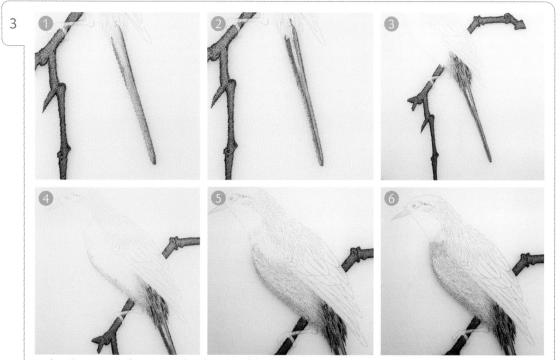

3

Embroidery Details for Step 3: The plumage of the kingfisher is rich in color. When embroidering, it can mainly be divided into three types: the entire vibrant feathers on the tail and wings; the soft, delicate feathers on the abdomen and neck that are more uniform in color; and the intricate, colorful long feathers above the tail and on the back. When embroidering neat plumage, ensure that the stitches are slanted at a significant angle. The stitches on both sides of the feathers should have a symmetrical feel. Begin embroidering from the outer sides towards the center line of the feather, finishing with the central portion. In figure 1, start by using a single strand of DMC 561# and 163# threads to embroider the dark green edge on the right side. Use DMC 163# and OLYMPUS 391# threads to embroider the turquoise edge on the left side. Then, use DMC 561# to connect with 163# and embroider from top to bottom on the right side. The left edge should be broader, while the right side is narrower. Within the right edge, use OLYMPUS 391# and DMC 518# threads to embroider from top to bottom. Following the color codes shown in the color diagram, after completing the tail feathers, start embroidering the fine, deep teal feathers between the tail and the wings. As shown in figure 3, begin by using a single strand of DMC 3799# thread as the base. Use long and short stitch with 3799# thread to create the deep gray areas, making the embroidered area slightly larger than the final appearance. Then, start from the lower right and use a single strand of DMC 163# thread to embroider long and short stitches in various densities according to the direction of the feathers. Next, use a single strand of OLYMPUS 247# thread to create some intermingling colors with long and short stitch between the two colors. For the middle section, start with OLYMPUS 386# thread and then blend in 391# thread for shading. At the top section, add 352# for shading. The fluffy feathers require alternating and interweaving of colors. Be careful not to rush the process. The abdomen is relatively straightforward, as shown in figures 4–6. Follow the thread color codes indicated in the diagram and embroider using long and short shaded satin stitch in the specified order.

4

Use the same method to complete the embroidery for the wings, back, neck, and head. For the eyes and beak outlines on the head, use stem stitch. After embroidering the main part of the bird's claws using single color long and short shaded satin stitch or blended (long and short) stitch, use a darker thread to slightly emphasize the edges with stem stitch on a few raised areas of the claws.

4

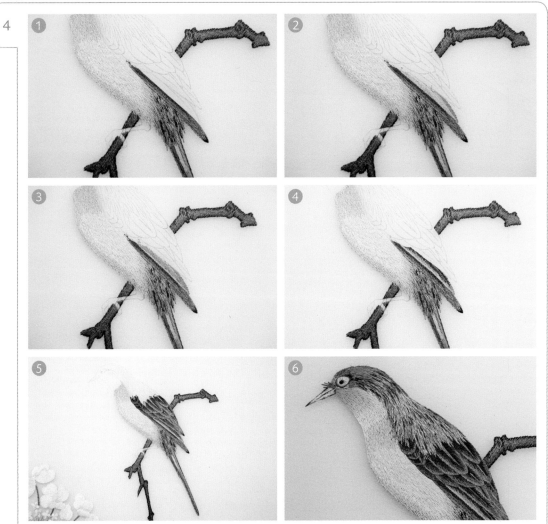

Embroidery Details for Step 4: When embroidering the wing feathers, work from the bottom layer to the top with long and short shaded satin stitch, making sure the stitches are slanted at a significant angle. Like the tail feathers, each wing feather should start from the sides, converging toward the center. The central line is embroidered last. After completing the wings, embroider the feathers on the back using the same technique as the fluffy feathers above the tail, paying attention to the overlapping threads and the sense of fluffiness. Next, continue embroidering the flesh-colored feathers on the abdomen, moving upwards until reaching the position of the beak. Then, embroider the teal feathers on the head. The head feathers should be smoother compared to the back feathers. Avoid making them too chaotic.